My Father, Fortune-tellers & Me

My Father, Fortune-tellers & Me

a memoir

EUFEMIA FANTETTI

Mother Tongue Publishing Limited
Salt Spring Island, BC
Canada

MOTHER TONGUE PUBLISHING LIMITED
290 Fulford-Ganges Road, Salt Spring Island, B.C. V8K 2K6 Canada
www.mothertonguepublishing.com
Represented in North America by Heritage Group Distribution.

Book Design by Mark Hand.
Wedding photo, p.9, March 16, 1968, Bonefro, Italy.
Photo Booth image on cover, 1974, Toronto, Canada.
Both photos found in the ruins of author's father's home during a trip to Italy in
August 2016. The house was damaged during the 2002 Molise earthquake.
Rider-Waite-Smith tarot deck images from *The Pictorial Key to the Tarot* (1910)
   (www.elfindog.sakura.ne.jp/pktset1922.htm)
Typefaces used: Cochin and Avenir
Printed on Antique Natural, FSC-Recycled.
Printed and bound in Canada.

Mother Tongue Publishing gratefully acknowledges the assistance of the Province
of British Columbia through the B.C. Arts Council and the support of the Canada
Council for the Arts, which last year invested $157 million in writing and publishing
throughout Canada. Nous remercions de son soutien le Conseil des Arts du Canada,
qui a investi 157$ millions de dollars l'an dernier dans les lettres et l'édition à travers
le Canada.

LIBRARY AND ARCHIVES CANADA CATALOGUING IN PUBLICATION

Title: My father, fortune-tellers & me : a memoir / Eufemia Fantetti.
Other titles: My father, fortune-tellers and me
Names: Fantetti, Eufemia, 1969- author.
Identifiers: Canadiana (print) 20190141115 | Canadiana (ebook) 20190141123 |
   ISBN 9781896949758 (softcover) | ISBN 9781896949772 (PDF)
Subjects: LCSH: Fantetti, Eufemia, 1969- | LCSH: Fantetti, Eufemia, 1969-—
   Family. | CSH: Authors, Canadian (English)—21st century—Biography | LCSH:
   Occultists—Canada—Biography. | CSH: Italian Canadians—Biography. |
   LCSH: Children of the mentally ill—Canada—Biography. | LCSH: Fathers and
   daughters—Canada. | LCGFT: Autobiographies.
Classification: LCC PS8611.A56 Z46 2019 | DDC C813/.6—dc23

for Cathy Sostad
sister soul

There was a star danced, and under that was I born.
Shakespeare

Write what should not be forgotten.
Isabel Allende

Search the darkness, don't run from it...
The moon appears for night travelers,
be watchful when the moon is full.
Rumi

CONTENTS

Tarot first appeared in Italy during the Middle Ages as a card game called *tarocchi*. The rules have been lost to history. At some point, the tarot deck transitioned into a tool for divination. Of the seventy-eight cards, twenty-two belong to the Major Arcana, (trumps, from the Latin for "triumph," *trionfi*). These represent the tale of a soul's progress, The Fool's Journey—a path with as many pressures as any hero's jaunt, but with a less prestigious name. The tarot, forged in medieval society with Western hierarchies and ideals, replicates our movement through life: spirits are born and swathed in innocence. We set out as wayfarers on a voyage strewn with trials, tribulations and triumphs. The search for meaning, the connections, the chaos, the disillusionment, the delights, the gratitude, the reckonings and the mercies, every fleeting epiphany of an examined life—the vast world of tarot contains them all.

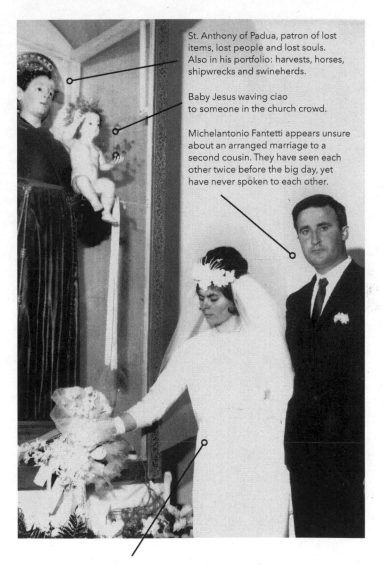

St. Anthony of Padua, patron of lost items, lost people and lost souls. Also in his portfolio: harvests, horses, shipwrecks and swineherds.

Baby Jesus waving ciao to someone in the church crowd.

Michelantonio Fantetti appears unsure about an arranged marriage to a second cousin. They have seen each other twice before the big day, yet have never spoken to each other.

Lucia Colombo holding the wedding favours—five sugared almonds wrapped in tulle: hope that the union will be more sweet than bitter. The Jordan almonds (confetti) symbolize health, wealth, happiness, fertility and longevity. My folks scored two out of five.

The Fool
(0)

The querent acts on instinct and sets out on a journey.

My father likes to say he was lucky, that God held both his hands and stopped him from killing my mother. Even Job, he notes, would have lost his infamous patience.

"Imagine if you had one parent in the jail, and another one under the ground." Whenever he muses on this, his Italian-accented English elongates every vowel in the first word to sound like he's pronouncing the name Imogene. He made the case for Divine Intervention again over the phone while I sorted through piles of clothes to pack.

I cradled the receiver against my shoulder and sighed. "Papa, please, that's a terrible example of good luck."

There is magical thinking involved here. He believes Jesus stepped in and worked behind the scenes as consummate theatre stage manager, ensuring we all played our parts, shielded from critics in the audience. This is the type of luck that led to rabbits having their feet amputated and used as accessories for keychains in the 1980s of my youth. The "Step right up and try your luck" of the carnival barker with guaranteed entertainment but no discernible winner. Everyone-quit-complaining-about-inequities-and-grab-a-bootstrap luck. Stop-looking-at-the-stars -while-lying-in-the-gutter and get-back-in-the-game luck. The luck of the draw, not the luck one could count on — which I once overheard aptly described at a billiard bar: If not for bad luck, there'd be no luck at all.

"Luck," from the late Middle English *lucke*, absorbed from the German. People bounce back faster from disappointment, roll with life's sucker punches better when they think they are favoured by chance. Lady Luck — the Roman goddess of fate and opportunity known as Fortuna — rarely smiled on my folks. She grimaced during their fast courtship (two weeks) and winced through their thirty-six-year acrimonious arranged marriage. Maybe she wiped her hands of them at the wedding, threw her hands up in the air in that classic southern Italian gesture: "What do you want from me?"

I'd venture to guess the only way she acted as benefactor for my parents' union at all was through their theme song: "O Fortuna," the opening and closing movement from Carl Orff's composition. Every time I hear the dramatic score in a film, from the first warning plea of the choir through to the steady whispering beat that builds to a frightening crescendo of cymbals and drums, I suspect that this song reverberated through my paternal grandmother Femia's heart as my future parents made their way through the village with a procession and got hitched.

My dad insists that the Lord watched out for him — is certain the biblical sky dignitary dealt the cards for the game of Scopa my father played throughout his life.

"And if I didn't marry the woman who ruined my life, I wouldn't have you. I got what I wanted in this world: someone I could talk to. I prayed for someone reasonable and I got you."

"Honestly, I think you could have held out for more, and it wouldn't have appeared greedy."

I've worried about my father for so long, permanent wrinkles have etched into my middle-aged forehead. The first nightmare I ever had, as a seven-year-old growing up in the west Toronto suburb of Etobicoke, was about my father in life-threatening danger. My parents had settled in the municipality of Alderwood, a sprawling working-class neighbourhood of carbon-copy bungalows. A smattering of trees dotted the cookie-cutter landscape of Thirtieth Street bordered by factories, highways and strip malls. In the strange setting created by my child psyche, my dad sat at a kitchen table on the lawn of a classmate's home, a girl who terrified me in elementary school. My father sat calm and serene, unmoving, as a gang of cartoon aliens attacked him—all replicas of the Great Gazoo from *The Flintstones*. My mother and I stood on the sidewalk while the animated extraterrestrials swarmed and hit him repeatedly. He took no notice. I called out to him and tried to wriggle free of my mother's grip. She refused to let go, ignored my pleas to help him. In the dream, I believed he would die. I stretched out my arms and screamed for him to watch out, to get up and to fight back. I shouted myself awake with a shrill, "Nooooooo."

The late summer light filtered in my bedroom window as my mother ran up the stairs from the basement kitchen. She burst into my bedroom with one hand on her heart, "O Dio, che cosa? Chè success?" I stifled my sobs. With my father at work, I was alone with her again. On mornings when my dad had already left for the factory, I moved anxiously, attentively, with apprehension, dread lodged in my stomach at the thought of making a misstep.

"Niente. Tenev nu mal sogno."

Mamma plunked down on the edge of my bed and smoothed the blankets. "And so? What happened in your bad dream?"

Before human ingenuity invented fire alarms, carbon monoxide detectors and earthquake warning systems, we had to gauge the danger of a situation using solely our bodies and brains. At seven, I couldn't predict the emotional atmosphere or potential for catastrophe with much accuracy. I stared at my mom, searched her face for signs of trouble: I tried to foresee how the day might unfold, whether her hazardous temperament would ignite or if she would hold down the home fort with calm. The change frequently happened instantaneously: a flicker of a frown before her dark brown eyes turned black. Her pupils appeared to eclipse the irises until I could see no distinction, and I would find myself cornered by an agitated shark.

I shook my head. She was one of the villains in the dreamscape. The real one in contrast to the cartoonish bunch.

"Tell me. You'll feel better."

"Some people were hurting Papa. He was dying."

My mom laughed and patted my legs under the covers. "That's good! That's a good omen! It means your father's healthy. The reverse of what you dream is true."

Doubtful, I squinted at her.

That day she stayed anchored to reality and made my favourite meal of pastina chicken soup for lunch.

Later at dinner, my father confirmed the same belief. "The village elders said the opposite of everything we dream is the truth. Don't worry. You should be scared if you dream I'm in good health."

Even then, as I watched my parents dig into their bowls of pasta fagioli, their advice felt topsy-turvy. Fruit Loops reasoning.

My parents rarely agreed on anything. My father was the embodiment of humble. My mother could be described as haywire. She held many bizarre assumptions: Being born on Christmas was so offensive to Baby Jesus, she said, that the person would suffer from lifetime lycanthropy and could never go outside during a full moon. Also: People lived in the walls of our home and had us under surveillance. Black people were black because God didn't like them and allowed them to be burned. Pointing at the moon during any of its phases, waxing or waning, caused warts, skin rashes and my future husband to become a hunchback.

I ran away to university on the West Coast as soon as possible—foolish enough to think I could outrun family trouble, presumptuous enough to hope everything that haunted me could be contained like radioactive waste back in that bungalow in Etobicoke instead of seeping into every area of my adult life.

Imagine my surprise. Learning the same lesson over and over again that travelers tripping around the world figure out fast—the same wisdom uttered by Buckaroo Banzai in the cult classic film: "No matter where you go, there you are."

Lucky meant living 3,000 miles away from my parents. Then, echoing my childhood nightmare, my dad nearly died for real. After twenty-two years away, I wrapped up my tranquil life in Vancouver to head back to my hometown of Toronto. I collected cardboard boxes and purchased a new suitcase. I also prepared by visiting a tarot reader and consulting an astrologer.

I came from a family that believed in fate, our destiny determined to such a degree that my dad and his sisters frequently offered this old chestnut with a world-weary sigh: it's already been written. Everything that has happened, is happening, will happen—past, present, future—has been predestined. We're all simply playing our roles, repeating our lines in this masterful spectacle: our actions, ideas and deeds following the prewritten script of the great big playwright in the sky.

This rankled my freewill heart, but I'd spent hours, weeks, years—two decades at least, maybe more—trying to decode the pattern behind the events, trying to anticipate all the possible outcomes, attempting to navigate the path ahead through prophecy: checking astrological aspects, documenting moon phases, getting my tarot read and reading my own, writing intentions at potent times, visiting a Vedic astrologer for a karmic report (nineteen years of a Saturn Dasha, the taskmaster planet of karma—my yoga teacher gasped), recording and deciphering every dream I could remember on waking. Especially taking note of my dreams. Because that first dream I had at age seven was accurate and prophetic: My father was in trouble. I knew it long before he did, but he eventually caught on.

The spiritual teacher Ram Dass once said, "If you think you're enlightened, go spend a week with your family." A week versus years, possibly the rest of my life: perhaps nothing could equip for this major shift.

My father's final words of advice to me as I packed? "Don't bring the cat. Leave him there in Vancouver with a friend."

"No. I'm not doing that—don't even try to talk to me about Figaro."

"So you mean if it's between me and the cat, you choose the cat?"

"Can you hear how ridiculous you sound?"

His older sisters got involved in our quarrel.

My Aunt Sofia: "What if something happens and the cat dies? Where are you going to bury a cat in an apartment?"

My Aunt Angelina: "You think we don't have cats in Toronto? They're all over the place here, like rats." She believed felines did the Devil's work as furry minions. My father and his sisters grew up in the aftermath of the Second World War. Their educations had been curtailed. Angie had probably learned about the sinister whiskered beasts spreading evil (and possibly Black Death) the old-fashioned way: from inaccurate stories passed down through oral history.

Others might argue this point, but there is no obstinacy like southern Italian stubborn. I left home so I wouldn't grow into a reed that bent to everyone's will—on my return, I refused to budge.

I bought Figaro a plane ticket, and stressed about getting the roly-poly twenty-two-pound feline into a carrier, checked in, and across the country. In the weeks leading up to our departure, I spoke to him about Hogtown cats sleeping as much as those in Terminal City. He would slink away to his food bowl without acknowledging me. I stockpiled catnip for the trip.

At the airport, a young man swabbed the contents of the carrier case I'd generously covered in cat cannabis. Figaro Amadeus Fantetti clung to me like a barnacle and caterwauled his distress to everyone travelling through YVR that morning, weighing in with his hefty opinion: "If cats were meant to fly, we'd have wings."

I called my father right before boarding, nerves frazzled, to relate the misadventure so far.

"Boy oh boy. What about the people who are allergic? What

are they going to do?"

"You think I should care about strangers more than my cat?"

"I didn't say that."

"Actually, you did."

"Let's not start a fight now when you're coming home."

In the past, we constantly fought about my mother. Now that he was divorced, and my mother lived as a ward of the province's Public Guardian and Trustee, we found other ways to needle each other. I desperately wanted to avoid my mother's grasp. I hadn't even boarded the plane yet, and already I was flooded with second thoughts. Useless. Why couldn't I have been blessed with second sight?

THE MAGICIAN.

The Magician

(I)

She searches for answers.

As soon as I learned to read, I yearned for words, sentences and stories every day, an infatuation that turned into a full-blown, lifelong love.

At age five, in kindergarten, other Italian kids would translate the missing vocabulary until I got the gist of Inglese. My reading comprehension was faster than my speaking. I tripped over my tongue to switch a thought from Molisan to English that wouldn't make people laugh at my pronunciation. The first difficult English word I learned to spell correctly was made up of three smaller ones: To + get + her. Our kindergarten teacher had spaced out the words, then she wrote the adverb out, conducting a symphony of characters on the chalkboard while I stared, spellbound by the letters as they appeared—one after another. We practiced sounding the syllables in unison one morning for a class on sharing playthings and playing fair. This was enchantment: the repetition was communion, the cursive

letters of the alphabet combining and joining like they had always known each other and never wanted to be left alone — the
whole stunning result a thrill for me; swiftly connecting defini-
tion to communicating ideas.

In grade one, I had grasped a thick red pencil and made
crude attempts to recreate the alphabet. Our teacher instructed
the class to copy her movements in majuscule and miniscule.
The paper had multiple lines, similar to sheet music, to offer
boundaries and direction for the curve in the lowercase *b* and
the mid-cutting line of a small *t*. During these early attempts at
composing letters, my own hand mesmerized me as its deliber-
ate motions formed barely decipherable letters across a page,
the giant *E*, the backward *f* and the malformed *m* of my name
making a proclamation in primitive childish print: I am here.

In order to tell a true story — one that is still sorting itself out,
still being lived — work with the Rule of Three: the principle
that every tale must have a beginning, middle and an end. In
Latin, *omne trium perfectum* — the idea that three is a complete set,
three achieves perfection. Julius Caesar understood the triad of
triumph when he wrote to the Roman Senate: *veni, vidi, vici*. The
tenet of Three-fold Law exhorts that any energy, good or bad,
an individual puts forth in the world is returned to her. Trios
dominate. A trapped fairy grants three wishes. The Three Magi.
The Holy Trinity. Mother, father, child. Birth, life and death.
Blood, sweat and tears. Rock, paper, scissors. Three square
meals a day. An appetizer, main course, dessert. Tricky business, finding an ending when part of the narrative is happening
in real time, being lived one day to the next, the plot elusive: a
mixed experience of minor revelations, repeated patterns of behaviour, and nudged memories. In our family, one crisis looked

much the same as the previous and had the same basic qualities as the next.

I puzzled over the saga that wove through our history — when was the seed of our curse planted? Where did the family illness start?

Two million years ago, frost buried Europe and North America under miles of ice and drove half the animal species on both continents into extinction. All of our ancestors showed up during a time of inclement weather 300,000 years ago, venturing out of Africa to anywhere that beckoned with the promise of survival. According to a test I purchased online, the family ancients wandered east through Asia Minor and Arabia, possibly setting up house and tucking in for generations before moving north again to collect one percent of Neanderthal genetic material — 45,000 years ago — approximately around the time those guys slid into disappearing, on the road to obsolescence. At some junction, prehistoric Scandinavians arrived, hunting, gathering, fishing and Viking into our Tree of Life.

Eventually, somebody decided to make a break for the boot-shaped landmass. I picture a long-gone relation creating that famous gesture for the first time: a hand under the chin and flipping the fingers outward to say he was fed up, finished with this frigid climate and fighting over scraps. Forget this lousy cold, I want my descendants to enjoy a cappuccino in about 10,000 years.

Around the same time, cows, chickens and sheep were domesticated in Southeast Asia and the Middle East. Every creature needed to sustain these carnivores was tamed, farmed or hunted, including goats, pigs and wild rabbits. Wheat they coaxed from the ground.

Roughly 5,000 years ago, writing systems appeared.

Assyrians and Sumerians began recording the oldest known references to individuals who possessed supernatural skill, the power to wreak havoc. With one inadvertent glance, these people could cause complete ruination, disaster or death. Women, children and livestock were considered vulnerable and required amulets for protection, and cures contained saliva and various sundries. Spilled salt also vexed the Sumerians, and they started the custom of throwing the crystalline dust over their shoulders to ward off catastrophe.

Legend contends that 2,760-odd years ago, Rome was founded by a warmonger who killed his twin brother over a location, location, location dispute. Romulus engineered the abduction of Sabine women during a festival in honour of Neptune to acquire brides for his soldiers—men given salt rations, an allowance to purchase the mineral because they were worth their weight in salt.

The Sabine men returned to Samnium, our ancestral homeland, declared war on Rome and armed themselves for battle. At first the Romans faltered, losing a pivotal fight. When Romulus's men gained the upper hand, the stolen women, now mothers of children born to Romans, braved the battlefield and rushed between their husbands and fathers, begging both sides to stop, beseeching the men to surrender and live in peace. This account—the Rape of the Sabine Women—repeatedly painted in oils and once carved in marble was considered an example of successful assimilation.

This is uncannily similar to the story about the beginnings of Bonefro—a village situated on a hilltop in Molise, one of the modern names for the ancient territory known as Samnium, a place that boasts a Lombard era castle, a sign that people fought and defended the region over 1,000 years ago. Here's the yarn: swap the epic Roman army for a small band of peasants on a pilgrimage to visit the sanctuary of Archangel Michael. Journeying with the group were three couples who wanted to consecrate their union. The hapless travelers camped for a night in the woods near Bonefro. Local shepherds kidnapped the women. Tra-a-a-dition. The distraught husbands, heard lamenting as far as the Heavens, were turned into boulders to cope with the pain and placed in a river named The Wailing Women. The wives wept so intensely their tears formed a new spring, another freshwater source, under the town. The Heavens took pity on the seized lovers and transformed them into three white doves. In other versions, the women stay human, and give birth to the first Bonefranis.

A bedtime story for the ages: amore, an arduous journey, and atrocity. If you're going to plagiarize an origin myth, you might as well choose the founding of the Eternal City.

Another fabrication: Gaius Pontius, a Samnite General, was the great-great-great-keep-counting grandfather of Pontius Pilate, the Roman procurator of Judea who ordered the crucifixion of Jesus of Nazareth to placate a mob. Those Romans: such crowd pleasers. Some say this historical begetter cursed the village descendants when he killed the Son of God.

But with everyone naming their children after themselves (a practice that continued — everybody has a brother/cousin/uncle called Tony), the name Gaius was common, and more than one Pontius clan proliferated through old Italy, like the surname Smith in the English-speaking world. My mother's equally plain maiden name — Colombo — can be found all over the Apennine range. She shares the patronymic of that famous Cristoforo, the man who bungled his way into discovering unknown lands and bullied his way to devastating Indigenous populations.

Three hundred and fifty-seven years ago, my father's surname shows up in the Bonefrani record books with the death of a thirty-year-old man, Don Giovanni Vincenzo Fantetti. So many options: the moniker could be the diminutive of the first name Fante, or may have started off as Fantetta, and could have been shortened to Fante. In Bonefro, two lines of the family emerge as distinct: the pious line bearing priests, and my father's ancestors—the bandits.

My dad is proud of this heritage: "These weren't bad persons. Not just go around shooting the people bang-bang for no purpose. They were bandits of honour. Men who turn away from the government because of corruption, because of poverty, and prejudice. Men who fought injustice because their families were starving."

Eighty-six years ago, a toddler, the first child born to my paternal grandparents, died the victim of *stregheria*—witchcraft. She developed a fever and faded until she was gone. Their second child, my eldest aunt, Sofia, also fell ill, her forehead and cheeks flush with heat. They found a woman who could perform the ceremony to remove the curse and rid Sofia of the affliction. She became my aunt's godmother, her protector. As an adult, my aunt will learn the treatment to eliminate *malocchio*, the evil eye, and use this antiquated remedy on me when I am six months old, cranky, fussy and hexed. With a bowl of water and several drops of olive oil, my aunt diagnosed and cured the malediction: irritable baby syndrome.

Eighty-one summers ago, when the sun was in Cancer, the sign of family, and the moon was in Leo (the lionhearted), my father, Michelantonio Fantetti, was born under a Fascist regime to poor parents. Prized by his grandfather, baptized with a blacksmith for a godfather, and touched by God's grace, he will survive the devastation on the horizon: another world war.

At six, he was nearly slaughtered along with his mother, aunt, cousin and grandmother by a group of retreating German soldiers. One frantically waved a rifle, ready to execute the women and boys until a comrade intervened.

At eight, his life was saved by the family dog, a German Shepherd, when it sprang forward and intercepted a viper about to strike.

What else should I tell about this rock, this North Star? He will pay off all his father's debts and put money in the bank. He will support the past and future generation through the grueling work of butchery, though he dreamt of becoming an engineer. A teacher will note his talent with numbers and ideas, and label him a born philosopher. He will model generosity and compassion when faced with envy and animosity. He will offer brief arithmetic lessons in the bracing air of the meat and poultry section of the supermarket.

He will convince child-me that he is capable of performing magic and stealing the nose off my face, until I spot his thumbnail. He will write cheques to purchase books through a Scholastic in the Schools program and never deny me a trip to a busy shopping mall bookstore. He will be a martyr in marriage and dawdle in despair where others would have sought a divorce.

He will keep a Ziploc bag full of salt taped to the door of his bachelor apartment to avert evil. He will give this advice often when I'm down on myself, "You should go look in the mirror and say to yourself 'Maybe I'm no the best, but I can't be the worst in the world' and then you feels better." He will provide this pep talk when I'm battling depression: "You no stealing. You no hurt nobody on the purpose. You no cheats the people. You no was kill nobody."

Setting the bar low works wonders.

THE HIGH PRIESTESS

The High Priestess
(II)

*She meets the keeper of the
eternal hearth and guardian of
her heart.*

The Christmas before I turned six, my parents pulled me out of kinder-class and we travelled to Bonefro. We would stay with my father's parents and visit my maternal grandparents.

Past my bedtime on the overnight Alitalia flight, my parents had grown sleepy and slumped in their seats, so I climbed over my father to find freedom and fame.

"Where you go? Don't be bother the people," he warned.

"I won't," I said, and sashayed up the aisle, hanging off armrests, batting my eyelashes like Darla in *The Little Rascals* — the Depression-era comedy films that aired before Saturday morning cartoons — blowing kisses to amused passengers.

I scampered around sing-shouting a repertoire of theme tunes from television programs like *The Friendly Giant* and *Mr.*

Dressup. I added lines from my favourite toy commercial: "It's Slinky, it's Slinky, fun for girls and boys!" I performed a medley, stringing the songs together and throwing in "la-la-la" to cover the lyrics I'd forgotten.

Elderly Italians en route to visit relatives smiled, the attention addictive. I wiggled around, copying a tap dance number I'd seen a chubby, freckled-faced girl perform on the TV series *Tiny Talent Time.* I performed a freestyle interpretative routine: a mash-up of movement that included jazz hands, giddy twirling and improvised summersaults. I tumbled several steps sideways when my father stuck his arm out and caught me by the waistband of my polyester hip-huggers, interrupting my show-stopping finale, "Can you tell me how to get, how to get to Sesame Street?"

"Basta. Sit down like good girl, or Nonna Femia will be upset with you."

His comment stopped me cold. "But she's not here," I said.

Though I had no memory of her, I idolized my paternal grandmother and felt jittery and jumpy about meeting the woman whose passport photo gazed on me with such kindness and love. I was her namesake, her youngest and last grandchild.

"She knows everything, including what's happening on this plane. People are trying to sleep, and you want to put on a show," my father said. "Sit and be quiet."

I crawled back into the spot between my parents, sniffling. I folded my arms across my chest, an imitation of my mother's frustrated with her lot in life pose, and shut my eyes. Five fidgety minutes later, I turned to my mother sleeping in the seat next to me and let out an exaggerated vaudevillian sigh. I couldn't fall sleep, and now worry pinged around my puny brain that I'd ruined Nonna's ability to love me by being too loud. I wanted to pester my father with questions about his mother's curious skill, but he'd settled back, eyes closed, arms crossed, end of discussion, end of my brilliant career entertaining passengers on board Alitalia. So much for a suitcase stamped with Paris, Tokyo, and Madrid.

I woke in my grandparents' bed to see my Nonna's round smiling face leaning over me, her silver hair pulled back into a firm bun. Dressed in a long dark grey skirt and black sweater, she sat, pillow-plump and with steady calm, beside me. She brushed hair away from my forehead and pulled the blankets back. I sat up in her bed, and she wrapped her arms around me, planting multiple kisses on my ear; I shrank back a little, shoulders hunched out of worry she might not like me, a feeling I'd picked up from my mother. Nonna's hug grew fierce and snug as I breathed in the woodsmoke smell of her clothes and the house. My body relaxed, knowing we belonged to each other: I clung to her for the duration of the visit. She had the saddest smile I'd ever seen, a replica of my dad's.

That first night in Bonefro, I fought off tiredness from the trip and time change, whining that I wanted to stay with Nonna, but my gruff grandfather would not be put out of a good night's rest. I stepped forward and left a cautious kiss on his hollowed cheek before heading to my own cot in a small corridor upstairs. I wouldn't allow anyone but Nonna get me into my pajamas. She tucked a Saint Anthony of Padua prayer card—her cherished patron of lost articles and travelers—into my pillowcase for protection.

The next morning, dressed and hair-combed to impress, I went downstairs, and a grey blur dashed for cover: a cat. A gift from my grandmother because my father had informed her of my feline-fanaticism. In Canada, I chased the ones I saw across the street, meowing after them, believing they could understand me, imagining our conversations in cat-tongue.

My father warned me not to approach the feral cats roaming the village defending their territory—they weren't the friendly Disney Aristocats I hoped to befriend.

The smoke-grey cat had olive-green eyes and hid from me when I called for it in Molisan, "Mousz-mousz? Mouszelle?" I sat on the floor next to the bed, biding my time for it to make an appearance.

"He's afraid." Nonna persuaded me off the ground with an apple slice.

"Afraid? Of what?" Kismet: my grandmother knew more about cats than I did. I munched on crispy fruit and followed Nonna to her favourite spot, a chair near the French doors that led onto a small south-facing balcony.

"It's 'of who,' dearest. He's afraid of you," she said. She lowered herself gingerly into the chair she often sat at by the window, ready to greet the sun. The light made her brown eyes the colour of caramel.

"Why is he afraid of me? I love him. Doesn't he know I love him?"

The cat darted for the front door, and I chased him, grabbing his tail and holding on hard. Picking him up in one scoop, I buried my face in his neck. He squirmed as I planted three loud smooches on him, before he broke free and leapt away.

Everyone except my grandmother yelled at me to stop kissing the fleabag. Nonna wiped my mouth clean, and removed the fur from my lips. She gently stroked my face with a thin hanky soaked with spit while I hummed and purred. We were a tribe of two: I perched on Nonna's lap and traced the wrinkles around her cheeks with my index finger. I leaned my back against her chest to burrow into her radiant warmth. She was the brightest star in my sky, with me content to run around her in circles like a spastic comet. As long as my grandmother was in the room, I was safe, my father was safe.

The trip erased my mother's perma-frown. She became gentle with me, taking my hand to help me down the cobblestone streets, holding tight while we crossed the piazza together, shielding me from the cold wind that wound through the village's sidewinding roads.

I was used to my mother pulling sharply, yanking me downstairs so hard I would fall and land in a heap at her feet. She would shout at my clumsiness, and slap me across the face for tripping this way and that, always underfoot, in the way, a nuisance. But in Bonefro, my mother fixed my hair with a tenderness I'd never experienced from her: she fastened barrettes and gave in to pigtail requests without losing her temper.

I could relax my guard.

Throughout the long winter visit, a month and a half, a feeling of tranquility ensued — a temporary truce between my parents — everyone on their best behaviour. Partway through that first visit, my father, for his own amusement, encouraged me to badger my grandfather for help with my broken hobbyhorse, a toy my parents purchased soon after we arrived in the village.

Afraid of Nonno's moody silence. I approached him tentatively, and used my hushed well-behaved voice.

"No," he said, frowning and shaking his head.

My father laughed.

I hid behind my grandmother's apron for the rest of the afternoon.

The next morning, the toy was fixed.

My grandfather, tall and skeletal, had a gaping mouth when he ate. He had one tooth left, a lonely lateral incisor yellowed with nicotine and tar from his sixty years of smoking, a habit he'd picked up as an eight-year-old boy. In his 30s, while stationed at Bari during the Second World War, he met a psychic and learned he would live to a ripe, comfortable old age, so he had no worries about his health. Presumably the psychic said nothing about caring for his fragile teeth.

Nonna Femia prepared boiled chestnuts for a treat: he could manage the softened insides mashed around his maw.

My grandfather caught me gawking at him as we ate.

"This tooth fell out too," Nonno said.

I winced. "Did it hurt?"

"Bah. I picked it up and pushed it back in. Told it to stay."

That tooth, and the story, transfixed me. After that, I trailed my grandfather around like a shadow, mimicking his postures whenever my grandmother was occupied.

In the neighbouring village of Casacalenda, Nonna bought my first talisman: a gold-chained necklace with a pendant of the Sacred Heart. More protection. She made meals of pasta and chickpeas over the hearth in a tiny cauldron. The glow of burning wood bewitched me. Every night, the dark of the Renaissance-rustic countryside closed in while we sat, safe and warm, in a semicircle by the fire. I cuddled up next to my grandmother and basked in her comforting, woolly-old presence, the opposite of my abrasive young mother.

La Befana, the crooked-nose crone who flew around on her broomstick on the eve of the Epiphany, left toys with my grandmother: a tiny copper cooking pot, a miniature coffee bean grinder and a small brass firepit. I stirred imaginary chestnuts in the pot and made invisible espresso for everyone.

My father threw back his pretend drink in one gulp. "Very nice."

My mother ignored the imperceptible cup and saucer placed in front of her.

Nonna sipped and smiled. "Good."

My grandfather chimed in, "Good if she learns now to make her future husband happy."

My father snorted with disgust. "Don't be backward."

Dad wanted an easier life for me, planned for my education to end when I wanted, not when the wallet was empty.

Three days before our departure, my mother carried me upstairs for my afternoon nap. I woke up after sunset and crept downstairs in darkness, feeling my way along the wall toward the fire-lit main level and the sound of my mother's voice. She sat across from my grandmother, plucking an upside-down chicken that my Nonna held grasped by its feet over a pan on the ground. It took a moment for my eyes to adjust, to realize that the chicken was headless and dripping blood that drained into the pan.

I screamed and startled them; my grandmother put her free hand to her heart. My mother leapt to her feet, tipping the contents of the pan over the floor.

I ran back upstairs and refused to come down for dinner. My grandmother brought me a plate over my mother's protests about spoiling me. One peek at the tomato sauce and I turned away, crying, to face the wall next to my bed. I refused Nonna's offer to prepare something else. She returned with chickpeas mixed with olive oil and plain pasta, and encouraged me to eat the safe beige meal.

I remember little about my maternal grandparents on this trip, except that their standoffish nature made me wary of them. On our last night in Bonefro, they came with other family and friends to pay their respects and say goodbye. My mom wept and nudged me forward to hug them. To my maternal grandparents, I was merely another girl. A drain that required a dowry. The daughter of their youngest daughter—they'd hastily arranged Mamma's marriage and happily sent her away.

The last night, one of the few times we were all together: my father's parents and my mother's parents. My mother's father, Nonno Baron, and my father's mother, Nonna Femia, were cousins. In her home that night, Nonna Femia offered hospitality to her cousin's cheerless wife, Nonna Sapooch—a woman with a remarkable capacity for cruelty and a knack for doling out maledictions.

I stayed awake as long as I could, wishing morning would never come. I followed Nonna Femia around like an orphaned duckling, not letting her out of my sight, longing to be left behind with her. My grandmother's presence, her gentle touch, softened an ache in my heart and healed the rift in my regular world. I wanted to stay in that old house, that cozy space and comfortable place, forever. I would fall asleep if I could be stranded there: a princess preserved for a hundred years in a fairy-tale kingdom, surrounded by the familiar, no longer a foreigner. Not the girl other kids made fun of because she wasn't fluent in English; not the child other kids singled out as different because she didn't understand the rules of engagement.

At the airport in Rome, we stood alone together. My mother and father watched our suitcases move along the conveyor belt—the three of us dejected Magi—going home to a country where I had citizenship and my parents did not.

On the flight back to Canada, I felt shy and subdued. I hummed a melody to myself, "Tu Scendi Dalle Stelle," an Italian Christmas carol. You come down from the stars/O King of Heaven, I crooned. My mother pinched my arm to shush me.

A stewardess leaned over us to shutter the window and blocked out the starry sky.

THE EMPRESS.

The Empress
(III)

*She collides with the archetypal
mother (reversed).*

Three years later, a month before my Holy Communion, Nonno Gennaro called from Italy. My grandparents had planned to reunite with us in Canada to celebrate my receiving the sacrament, but Nonna Femia had woken that morning slower, weaker, her joints creaking. By nightfall, she was bedridden.

My father and his sisters raced to Rome. From Leonardo Da Vinci airport, dad called with the sad news that she had died during the night.

"Oh, ma no—" cried my mother. She sank into a chair and wailed. I lay on the ground, arms and legs stretched and swinging as if I could make a snow angel on the tiled kitchen floor. I stared at the ceiling, willing her back to life, bargaining with my Guardian Angel. He could have my mother instead, or take me to the afterlife as well. I didn't want to exist in a world without Femia.

Two years on, as a tender-hearted ten-year-old, I still ached over her loss. It didn't help that grade five was a Darwinian nightmare. Our teacher, Mr. Mayors, also the vice-principal, assured us that Regan would kick Jimmy Carter's ass on election day south of the border and retrieve those hostages from Iran pronto. He had the personality of an army tank, and hollered at me to "speak up" whenever I gave an answer in class, yet he signed all the photocopied class project yearbooks with a cheerful "Rise and Shine in '79"—a sentiment at odds with his intimidating demeanor.

Constantly disgruntled, he never spoke below the volume of a drill sergeant and barked questions at students. He wore tinted wire-rim glasses, the kind 1970s serial killers wore. Mr. Mayors once overheard a student call him Four-eyes, and once is all it took to get on Mr. Mayors' bad side. No one had ever found evidence of his good side, so we all persevered through purgatory at Douglas Park Elementary. We cowered while Mr. Mayors stood over us, snapping his yap chewing Aspergum because we were a headache.

His vitriolic style was one reason I disliked going to school. Denise MacDonald, the class bully, was the other. She hated me and singled me out for special attention on the playground at recess.

Once, crammed against the gym doors and squirming to break free, I yelled, "What is wrong with you? Pick on someone your own size."

Denise had failed grade five. A blonde-haired giant, she towered over the other girls and boys by six inches.

She pulled me forward to shove me again. With blue eyes as cold as her toothy smile, she taunted. "You like disco, don't you, freak?"

"I do. What's it to you?"

Her mouth fell open. "Are you a dummy?" She let go and turned to the throng of students who had gathered to watch. "She admits she's a freak." She walked away defeated: my admission had drained her potential fun.

I painted a permanent target on my back for her when I raised my hand in class and asked to write another speech for English class: in essence, I put in a request to finish more homework. I'd already completed a presentation on cats, fulfilling the assignment requirements. But paging through a book with holiday craft projects, the topic I should have chosen captivated me: witches.

Late in autumn on a Saturday afternoon, I sat at my desk and wrote down everything I knew about witchcraft on jumbo index cards. I revised the content and practiced in front of the mirror: "Mr. Mayors, boys and girls, my subject today may give you goosebumps." I kept to the five-minutes-and-under guideline.

The following Monday, Mr. Mayors announced that oral presentations were over unless someone felt they had something vital to impart.

Distracted by my classmate Rosa—busy telling me that my cards, written in my favourite purple ink, made me a "weirdo" in her eyes, and "gay"—I failed to raise my hand immediately.

When I did, waving like a frenzied air traffic controller, the Sargent-serial-killer made an ever-so-slow turn toward me. The students did the same s-l-o-w m-o-t-i-o-n pivot.

Mr. Mayors' jaw twitched. "Why weren't you paying attention? Is there someone else you should be listening to when I'm talking?"

Rosa's ears pinked and then her cheeks followed, the colour

enveloped her face much like a mood ring would bleed to the next shade.

"No. I'm sorry, Mr. Mayors."

"Come up here, then. Let's hear what you've got. Everyone put your books away. Let's give Eufemia our full and complete attention. Again."

Denise whispered, "Spaz," and a nervous giggle fluttered through the room like an outbreak of contagious cooties.

The goal to dazzle them with my detailed research fizzled. Black cats as familiars, spell casters, witch dunking—no one in Alderwood thought the subject as groovy as I did, evidenced by their bored expressions. A few kids perked up when I mentioned the test determining whether someone was a sorceress involved drowning to prove one's innocence.

Italy didn't have a Santa Claus, I informed them, but La Befana, an old woman who flew around on a broomstick delivering gifts on the eve of the Epiphany. She came down through chimneys and left presents with the family matriarch, the grandmother—the wise woman whose love was fiercer, more formidable and therefore more capable of offering protection from monsters than a mother's.

At recess, I shuffled over to girls hanging out near the monkey bars.

Nancy spoke first: "You're such a freak."

Rosa agreed. "Why are you a weirdo? Don't you like normal things?"

"What's wrong with witches?" As an only child, I was forever trying to read a group, a room or a situation after I'd already said or done something that made me stand out in an unfavourable way. And I never caught on, never got the gist, never solved the puzzle of not fitting in.

This led me to believe the problem was simple—it was me: I was the misfit.

Hours later, my father found me hiding out in the garage. Perfumed with motor oil and charcoal briquettes, our large garage acted as a hub, where every September, my dad made wine with his brothers-in-law. For a few years, I collected and stacked the wooden crates into a wall in the far corner of the garage, telling everyone it was my new house. I assembled enough cartons to build a side and front wall four feet high, with a wide opening for the entrance. I kept treasures—a yo-yo, a *Richie Rich* comic and a penny—on the wall's interior makeshift bookshelf. And craving solitude to a greater extent than I feared creepy-crawly insects or grime, I placed my floral, kid-sized folding chair in the middle of the space, far enough away from spider webs and black ants. Most days I sat in silence until light from the windows grew dim, until my mother insisted I come inside or put on a jacket, or until one by one, my dad removed the crates to use as kindling for the wood cook stove in the basement.

That day, my dad sat down next to me at the picnic table he'd brought indoors for the winter. "What's happen?"

"Niende."

"Ca cose a scuol'?"

I buried my face in my hands. Nosy (the stray black cat I'd lured inside with tuna fish in a makeshift tin foil bowl) butted my arm. My parents had banned the cat from ever entering the house, and forbade pet ownership in general. They could not accept the idea of a cat or dog as companion. For my folks, all animals satisfied a particular purpose that served humanity: guarding the farm, killing the mice, transporting the grain, tilling the field, becoming part of the pasta sauce.

"Papa, m'a dimme ch'è success?" An odd language quirk from our region: my father called me Papa, the same way my mother called me Mamma. A role reversal in the terminology of relation that neither of my parents could explain. The switched honorifics served as a reminder of my responsibility in the family—a constant negotiator between the world my parents left behind in Bonefro and the new terrain of Toronto—adult duties rested on child shoulders.

"Nu'shun me piace." Nobody liked me. Before my father could offer a platitude, I sobbed out the truth. "Everybody at school laughs at me, not even behind my back but to my face. Everyone thinks there is something wrong with me. They think I'm strange."

What I didn't say, didn't have the vocabulary to voice then: Who could fault them?

My father peered out the window and back at me. His forehead creased—three evenly spaced lines from a Hilroy notebook to practice cursive—and nodded.

"What if I make filet mignon on the barbecue? You can be invite some friendly over to come for dinner."

Food: The cure-all for every ailment that dared to trouble Italians and their descendants. Generations subjected to poverty, exploitation, war, invasion and humiliation—all that anguish, supposedly erased with a hearty meal. People suggest food is love: not true. Food is food and love is love. Preparing a meal for loved ones is an act of devotion, and our stomachs had acclimatized to my mother's meals: nightly offerings of scorched green peppers, boiled chicken, bland watery tomato sauce that left the pasta noodles a pale mess in our bowls. She reused olive oil until it turned rancid. Sporadic evenings we ate edible nourishment when my father tired of the slop. He'd march into the garage on a mission and barbecue dinner: sausage seasoned with fennel, the best cuts of beef. He'd trained and mastered butchery in Switzerland, leaving as a Carnivore Encyclopedia. Meat was always the first remedy in his medicine cabinet.

His suggestion thawed the sadness that clawed at my chest, but a spark of anger ignited in its stead. "Did you hear what I said?"

"Everybody has to eat."

I shouted at him to go away, to leave me alone, that he couldn't fix this mess with offers of tenderloin. For the first time, I suspected that my father wouldn't be able to help me navigate life at all. I would have to figure things out alone.

After the stultifying school year ended, I set up a magic corner of the basement. My oasis.

In the centre was a mini-picnic table, a gift from my father. The day I brought home my final report card, we went to Canadian Tire and came back with this coveted piece of decor—an item I had stared at several times while accompanying my dad on his errands. He'd noticed. "You want? Bring home a good report card, and I'll get it for you."

The furniture I picked out for myself was a light wood colour, and it lacked the fake gold trim, or faded Euro-chintz style my parents favoured. Our main couch was upholstered in a combo tangerine and muddy brown scheme with the repeated pattern of an 18th century Romeo and Juliet. My picnic table eschewed plastic. I saw it as the centrepiece of a glamorous urban life.

"Where did you get this fabulous table? It's très chic and magnifique," future dinner guests would exclaim as I smiled, tossed my perfectly straightened hair and proudly trotted out speciality dishes learned from my *Nancy Drew Cookbook* with all its "Clues to Good Cooking," praise-winning recipes like The Case of the Smothered Pork-Chops and Spider Sapphire Spiced Cherries.

"Darlings, it's been in the family forever," I'd reply. "That rustic piece came from Canadian Tire."

My corner provided a cool reprieve from the heat. A combination of a hideaway and my childhood idea of an office, a command central for all my ambitions. Every day I entertained notions of becoming a famous jump-rope skipper or Hula-Hoop record breaker. Perhaps I would make a name for myself as an internationally renowned ghost-catcher, or as the world's foremost expert on Archie Comics, winning the Nobel Peace Prize for my work lecturing on the delicate balance between Betty and Veronica, affirming the necessity for harmony to prevail between blondes and brunettes.

I sat at the picnic table every afternoon and daydreamed that one day my real family, the one that abandoned me on this planet would come back for me. No doubt a cosmic catastrophe had held them up. I discovered my alien identity while watching the televised Disney movie *Escape to Witch Mountain*. Forget regular sorcery, this was next level: the struggle embodied by extraterrestrial siblings Tony and Tia echoed my very existence; I too felt caught in a world where I didn't belong, as the movie trailer announced. I would bide my time on Earth developing my telekinetic skill until my clan from outer space returned. I imagined how proud they would be when I slammed doors or hurtled lamps and toasters across the room without even blinking.

The first girl I managed to coax into hanging out at my new headquarters, Nancy, drew back and glared at me when I told her my secret identity.

I lowered my voice to a whisper for the reveal: "I'm a witch."

"Shut up. Are you retarded?"

I showed her a jar of pastel-stained eggshells saved since Easter and implied that the shells had mystical properties. I showed her my Barbie perfume maker. Any supportive friend could see that water, combined with a stick of solid pink rose-scented air freshener cranked into a tiny bottle equalled an elixir for the lovelorn. My collection of jam jars filled with saccharine-smelling concoctions, coloured water fragrances called Spring Fresh and Gardenia, were obviously love potions, potent remedies I had created to assist the lonely and loveless. I presented them to Nancy as jars of homemade eau de toilette.

She shook her head. "What is wrong with you?"

"What's wrong with you?" I mimicked to repel her doubt, refusing to let her shatter my personal spell. I wanted her to believe that I was extraordinary, blessed with extrasensory perception.

She didn't.

I willed the closet door beside Nancy to open into her face and send her reeling.

It didn't.

We sat at the table and flipped through books and comics. We agreed Richie Rich's position as the littlest rich boy in the world would be amazing and wondered why he always wore the same clothes when he was so wealthy. We both felt sorry for Charlie Brown, though Nancy came right out and called him a loser.

Nancy read the Peanut Gang antics while I made a sign on a scrap piece of cardboard with my black jiffy marker: Advice 10¢. I planned to dole out words of wisdom—psychiatric help plus sorcery assistance—a double double toil and triumph consultation.

Nancy laughed. "Do you think anyone would pay you a penny for your thoughts?"

"It's my Lucy sign. I can listen to people's problems and help. I'm good at that. I do it for my dad."

"Your dad asks you for advice? Give me a break." Nancy huffed and blew her bangs off her forehead. "No one is going to give up their allowance for your guidance." She rebuffed my offer of free counselling.

My mother came downstairs with that cold, wild-eyed look, obsidian and inscrutable, a frightening combination of vacancy and hostility that always made people step back or away. She stood in the doorway, blocking our exit.

I kept my voice calm while my insides fluttered with warning adrenaline. "Yes, Ma? Do you need something?"

She answered in Italian. "Tell this gypsy to get home."

"I have to go." Nancy said and didn't move.

I bit the inside of my cheek and answered them both, "Okay." We stood up together, and walked toward my mom in matching steps.

She turned sideways to let us through and grabbed my forearm, squeezing hard.

I tried my everything-is-fine smile for Nancy, but my mother's grip made me wince. A parody of a grin was the best I could do as I wrenched my arm back.

Nancy backed away from us until she reached the stairs. Then she turned and fled, calling, "See you later, alligator!" The screen door banged shut behind her.

I eyed the bottom step. Darting past my mother, I made it as far as the landing before she caught up with me. She backhanded the top of my skull. I fell forward, nose slammed into the glass screen door, and smacking it hard with my forehead. She jerked me down the stairs again and around the basement kitchen as she searched for a wooden spoon.

She ranted, "You send a spy signal to that gypsy's parents. You betray your own mother. Did you think you could fool me? I'll teach you the lesson you never learn in school and one you never forget. You think I don't know what you do? You think I don't know you're a whore? I know. I know everything. I catch you, slut. You live between your father's legs. You'll be sorry."

In a fury, she broke the spoon across my thighs.

I howled. "Ferme, Mamma, please stop—ne lo fatte. Ho fatte niede. I didn't do anything—mi fai male!" I begged for mercy and scrambled to get away from her blows. I curled into a fetal position and waited for her to exhaust her rage.

She screeched accusations of my affairs and divided loyalties.

My father heard us from the far end of the yard and came running. Coiled on the floor with forearms bracketing my head for protection, I glimpsed the blur of his legs as he raced past the basement window.

He yanked mother off me by the scruff of her neck. She fell sideways, and landed in a heap on the floor. Her head ricocheted off the side of the stove.

My father surveyed the damage and shrieked. He reached out and grabbed my arm to pull me up. I flinched and whimpered at his touch. My skin burned: every part of my arms and legs mottled with blossoming bruises that seared.

He bellowed his dismay. "What kind of mother are you? You're a monstrosity. A savage. A rabid animal that should be kept in a cage."

He struck my mother one, twice, and a third time before he heard my faint voice calling out for him to stop.

"Papa, fermeti. Please, please, no — "

My mother fought back: snarling, she kicked and swiped at his crotch.

I struggled, slick with sweat, to get on my feet. "Papa, ne iute niede." I knew punishing her helped nothing.

"O Dio. O Dio. Dio Sante. Ma c'ame fa? Dio, dimme. How are we supposed to live like this?" He helped me stand.

I limped upstairs, leaning against his frame for a crutch. My body couldn't stop trembling for hours.

THE EMPEROR.

The Emperor
(IV)

She observes the protector who was unable to provide.

Nonno Gennaro sauntered into our backyard through the side gate door. He'd emigrated at the insistence of his adult children after Nonna Femia died. He lived with Aunt Angelina until her family moved farther into the burbs of Mississauga, and then he settled in with Aunt Sofia's family, ten houses down the street from us. He roamed the space between the two homes smoking, searching for a glass of wine and a Scopa player.

From under the shade offered by latticed grape vines, already wilting in the muggy August morning, I sat staring at the grass. I wore a long-sleeved T-shirt that came to my wrists and roomy joggers with elastic cuffs at the ankle. My arms and legs throbbed, covered in rainbow welts that varied from marbled yellow to deep purple and black. In the centre of multiple bruises, the skin had broken altogether: blood seeped through and had dried to form a copper hue. Every movement—sitting, standing, strolling, getting into bed, getting out of bed and getting dressed—caused waves of stinging pain.

Nonno evaluated the vegetable garden and examined my father's handiwork before turning to scrutinize me. "Why are you dressed for cold weather in this heat?"

My father kept his gazed trained on the cucumbers and zucchini. He watered the greens and said nothing.

I balanced on the armrest of the chair to get up and give my grandfather a kiss.

"Why are you walking like a spider somebody stepped on?"

"I fell down."

Nonno shook his head. "State attente."

My father jerked his chin toward us. "So? Are we talking now? Like that, whenever it suits you?"

My dad and Nonno Gennaro had long been engaged in a fight. One that started in my father's boyhood when he laboured hard, loaned out to villagers to till their wheat fields with a sickle and transporting wood daily to their homes while Nonno drank and racked up debt. The slings and arrows of an impoverished youth led to much chaos. Nonno juggled vices, failed at managing money and took a casual attitude toward work.

"One puffy cotton-ball cloud in a clear blue sky and Nonno decided it was an omen forecasting bad weather." My father couldn't hide the frustration in his voice when he spoke of the past.

Their own rented fields left largely untended, Nonno let his three children go hungry to feed his compulsive cravings; as a girl, my Aunt Angelina sold or traded eggs the siblings needed for nourishment for her father's tobacco. At school, she once received the strap for not handing in her notebook of lessons at the end of the year. The book was destroyed when my grandfather used the pages as rolling paper. My father, turned away from mandatory army service at eighteen because he was deemed underweight and malnourished in his six-foot, 110-pound frame, struggled to contain his annoyance in front of me.

Nonno cleared his throat and spit. "Don't soak the ground. Might rain."

"You want to tell me how to grow plants? Because you did this work yourself and now you're an expert."

I hobbled away from them mid-argument and came back with homework Nonno had helped me complete in the last year of elementary school. I'd sketched a family tree on bristol board with leaves in shades of forest, emerald and lime green. On each leaf I wrote the names of coupled ancestors. For my mother's family, the Colombos, I could fill in one row of great-grandparents and a few scattered names with question marks beside them. But with Nonno's help, I'd extended the patriarchal line back five generations.

"Here." I handed the rolled-up artwork to Nonno.

He removed the elastic and sat down. "Hold it open for me." He reached for another cigarette.

My dad shut off the hose and joined us.

I had successfully brokered another temporary peace treaty.

"Tell me this story again." I pointed to the top of the tree. "Your nonno's nonno. My great-great-great grandfather."

Ever ready to spin a yarn and be the centre of attention, he took a long drag and launched into the chronicle of Michelangelo-the-felon who evaded capture, a man who killed a captain for disrespecting his daughter-in-law.

"He was an expert hunter," Nonno said. "Exceptional, the kind everyone knew about. Able to split a string from a distance."

"A string? I thought it was a hair." Certain elements of the tale were familiar because my father also loved repeating the story. A gallant murderer? Tough for any of us to resist.

Nonno hacked a cough, dislodging smoke-saturated phlegm in his throat. He spat again. "A hair? Who could see a strand of hair? That doesn't make sense."

I shrugged. If I interjected too often, he would refuse to talk.

"Each time he bagged a wild rabbit, he would send half to Captain Santoianni as a show of respect. His daughter-in-law would deliver the animal. She was young, beautiful and dutiful. One day she told her father-in-law, 'You go. I don't want to.' He said to her, 'What? Did the captain say something to you? Did he try something?' because in those times, honour was honour.

"Early the next morning, at five, the mules loaded with plows and seeds, Michelangelo gave his son instructions and settled down to wait. He took care to ensure he had a prime spot, and shot the captain of the gendarmes as the man passed in front of the Church of San Nicola."

"A foot chase ensued, shocked officers in pursuit of our ancestor while people in the piazza screamed: 'Michelangelo Fantetti shot Captain Santoianni! Captain Santoianni is dead!' They caught up to the marksman who said, 'You all have children as do I. I would be sorry if you left your children in the middle of a road, stranded without a father in this life, but you'll leave them there this morning if you pursue me. Resign yourselves and go. You won't take me.' The officers, who all knew the story of his sharpshooter aim and the string struck from a fair distance, walked away."

"And he didn't go to jail." I knew this was a favourite part of the story for both my dad and Nonno.

"For eighteen years, he lived in a cave and dodged the law—eighteen years, the police came to the village once a week from the capital city, and his friends would tell him to hide out in a cave bordering his farm.

"One day, tired of hiding, he stepped out into the piazza on an official police business day. He was spotted by a young officer who didn't know that this gracious, likeable fugitive from justice had been kept safe by another officer of the gendarmes; someone who admired Michelangelo and understood this 'family honour is the only honour' business. The young man shouted, 'There he is!' and fired a fatal blow.

"His family took him back to the farm to die next to the land he'd worked hard to maintain. His cop friend arrived and said, 'What were you doing? I told you to stay out of town today.'

"Michelangelo responded, 'Knives fair, knives different.'"

"Or possibly "Knives proud, knives shamed," my father interrupted. With dramatic flourish, dad finished the story. "What it means is: 'I killed a man. A man had to kill me. This is the death I was meant to have.'"

Nonno frowned, his finale stolen.

My father broke the awkward silence that followed. "You want a beer?" he asked, and without waiting for a response, he went indoors to get a couple.

While he was inside, my mother came through the gate, home from Mass. She spotted Nonno.

"What are you doing here, old goat?" Sounding suspicious in a way that made my breath catch, "What are you two talking about? He can't stay for lunch, so better if you stop talking to him now."

"Me'ne vie. I was leaving." Nonno leaned over and squeezed my knee.

I winced. My eyes welled.

He stared.

"What are you waiting for? You were leaving."

"Papa's here," I said. "He's inside." She wouldn't dare dismiss Nonno in front of his son.

She glared at me and stomped past us into the house, the screen door slamming like a rifle shot behind her. Moments later she shouted, broadcasting her misery to the neighbourhood; fed up with her lot in life, she bellowed at God to grant her the strength needed to put up with our idiocy before she lay in a coffin, slain by the circle of stupidity that surrounded her. "Auite, Dio, m'auite. O Dio, damma a forze. Questi scemi m'uccidano."

My father joined in her cacophony: "O per l'amore di Dio. He can't hear you, beast. God doesn't help the devil. Didn't they teach you that in church this morning?"

Nonno tried again. "Ch'è te success? Why do you walk like a broken creature?"

"Niende. Ho cadut."

He frowned. "Stat'e attente."

Many years later as an adult, decades after Nonno died, I revisited the story of Michelangelo with my father. I took notes, transcribing the cinematic moments of my long-ago ancestor's death. The history and the details became an obsession. I filled a few notebooks, and then a few more, adding a sentence, quibbling with my dad over exact wording and occasionally giving up when the accurate term couldn't be determined.

Some say ancestors need to be placated. During yoga classes, teachers said, "This practice heals up to seven generations back." Lying on a mat in Savasana, the corpse pose, one of the hardest to master, my thoughts would drift to my maternal and paternal grandparents: the good, the bad and all the ugly that passed between them. Time travelled in two directions though: seven generations back and forward. One mild sunny day in January, weeks after working on the translation with my dad, I woke with a voracious craving for a cigarette. My thirst for a drag was inexplicable — in a room with smokers, my throat constricted and eyes watered. I'd cough and move away. Other than a brief failed attempt to be cool at sixteen, I'd never smoked. I couldn't even approximate realistic smoking for the role I played as a pregnant bridesmaid in *Tony 'n' Tina's Wedding*. The cast and audience thought I did a wretched job of faking it, and several actors tried to teach me how to appear to puff like a pro. Casual and cool. I never pulled it off.

The hunger, the hankering wouldn't quit. I walked to the corner store and asked for cigarettes. The clerk said I needed to be specific.

"A pack of the smallest amount you sell."

"Which brand?"

"The one with an image of a camel."

Nonno Gennaro was a walking air freshener for Camels. The Turkish tobacco blended with American clung to his old blazer. I wasn't thinking about him. I wasn't writing about him. Then he made his presence known, and I did my best to honour his request despite the health risk. I lit one up at home and, after a couple of drags, put it out and kept the half-smoked cigarette on my table.

Alone in my apartment, I spoke aloud to the man who'd been dead for twenty-six years. "I've missed you, Nonno, but ask for tea with lemon when you want to stop by."

I gave the rest of the cigarettes away to a friend. I reasoned if Nonno visited him seeking the comfort of his earthly habit, my Canadian pal wouldn't understand the dialect.

Then maybe everybody could be happy.

THE HIEROPHANT

The Hierophant
(V)

She walks the bridge between this plane and other worlds unlocked by dreams.

The Centers for Disease Control and Prevention's website contains links to multiple studies published in journals about the potential impact of scoring high on an ACE test, not a test anyone wants to ace. The acronym stands for Adverse Childhood Experiences, and the first time I took it, I could imagine legions of female forerunners standing behind me, sneaking glances, exchanging looks and commenting on my answers.

"Look at this. She thinks she had it rough."

"Didn't she start working at sixteen? I'd already had two kids and a third on the way by then."

"She rises at seven, makes coffee and reads the news? Does she know we buried our own children?"

Embarrassed by my privileged, almost self-indulgent life

as a writer, I shut down my computer and went to the park. I watched the weekend farmer's market set up, and wished the genetic memory of grafting fruit trees, growing tomatoes and baking bread had been passed down as easily as the tendency to develop diabetes.

There is a vestige of ice that never melts, stays in a state of permanent winter, hibernating in the bodies of people who have endured harsh circumstances. Whether the remnant is lodged in their hearts, minds or kidneys is another matter. No doctor can pinpoint that frozen spot by x-ray or an MRI, but I suspect that the shred lurks in people everywhere, in their tendency to contrast suffering, carve notches into a desert island palm tree, count the obstacles in place, note what has to be overcome: lack, miserable surroundings, poverty, an absence of love and nurturing, betrayal or abandonment. In these stories we tell ourselves and others, we should proceed with caution and forgo comparison. The potential pitfall is that we become enamoured with the self-made myth and discount serendipity. "Look what a person can do," we say, "all on their own, if they try enough, work enough, are good enough."

Does anyone genuinely feel safe, buffered or prepared for the unexpected? Wealthy people who grew up poor think the wolf is still lingering near the entrance, waiting for one mistake to pounce and put them back in a perilous situation.

Violence is a virus passed down through generations; no one is immune to its effects. There are no antibiotics. The changes made to DNA, established neural pathways, competent modes of coping, altered brain chemistry are a riddle science will solve one day. The gamble, by which I mean the winning lottery ticket—finding or building a safe, stable home environment, means you did it despite the odds, with the deck stacked against you. The past is always clamouring to be heard in the present and attempting to weigh in with an unwanted opinion on the future.

TST: Trauma Standard Time, the result of growing up in a home or culture steeped in brute force, is as pervasive and persistent as the common cold. Symptoms include growing accustomed to head-jerking slaps and still feeling their sting years later. Living with random regularity: the constant chaos of the world, the change-is-constant factor of our universe, the tilt of the Earth's axis. Our bodies spinning through space on a bigger body turning in the cosmos—living with the unpredictable and still trying to forecast the future.

On the day I discovered the ACE test, I decided to use it for a lesson plan linked to an article on the problematic language around addiction (sticks and stones our ancestors fought with to survive, and we now use labels to tell people their value, to indicate their worth). I clicked through all the stages and scored what amounts to a C+ in academia and an "Oh, no" in the real world.

That night, I tossed and turned until two in the morning. In the brief window of sleep, the three hours before needing to get up and get gone to make it to campus on time, I had one of the dreams that has stalked me through adult life: I never left home. Never escaped the bungalow in Etobicoke. On waking, I splashed cold water on my face to shock the details out of my mind. At least, I mused on transit, I didn't repeat the upsetting one about my parents expecting another child.

At some stage growing up, while my brain was storing memories and sorting through experiences, cataloguing information, it must have called a production meeting and hired a director, a script consultant, a camera assistant and a set decorator to prepare for late-night viewing that persistently surfaced when I stressed. TST ticktocking in the background like a cuckoo clock.

In the worst recurring dream, my parents had another baby and I'd snuck into the house to kidnap the kid. I rarely made it down the creaky hallway to the front door before waking up, shaking and sweating, relieved that none of it was true — that my parents weren't so thoughtless, that I wasn't an insta-mom responsible for another human's happiness or well-being. Some nights I woke clutching a pillow — the babe I intended to steal.

In the other dream, I still lived at home, but worked at my current job, or the folks populating the dream were all people I'd met after leaving home. The nightmare machinations meant we were all stuck in my Etobicoke reality. Each time I had the dream, I would think, "How can this be? I thought I was done with this part of my life." In my journal, I recorded the second dream again, full of the Vancouver cast of friends, three months before moving back to Toronto.

In the realm of REM sleep, both my father and I brooded that we would have to relive the worst, endure the hassles, the legal battles and the trouble all over again.

He had two recurring dreams. In the first, though separated in 2004 and divorced in 2008, he remained married to my mother, and he had this ongoing matrimony dream again before I returned to Toronto.

In the second dream, stranded in Bonefro, he relived a dreadful time from his life. Bad weather had trapped him on a mountain pass, fighting with a mule to return to the shelter of the village.

The first time I heard this one, my jaw dropped. "You serious? You, the mountain pass and a donkey? I don't know what the word for cliché is in Italian."

The chore of collecting firewood meant a sixteen-kilometre hike to the woods round trip, and my dad did the route three times daily, three days a week in winter. Half the wood sustained the family through the snowy season, fuel for warming the house and cooking; the rest my dad sold to purchase sustenance. "Forty-eight kilometres a day of walking. From the time I was a young teenager until I went to Switzerland when I was 21."

Me, the city slicker raised in a house with electricity, running water and a furnace, I asked the dumb question: "Wouldn't it have been better to do it all at once?"

"You can't overload a donkey, it will collapse. The donkey falls down, how can you bring home wood to stay warm at night?"

The donkey, Serpent, belonged to another villager. My father borrowed the animal daily. Once, during a particularly bracing winter, the wind through the mountain pass blew bitter and harsh. My father felt his skin prickle with frostbite. He wore weathered old shoes, threadbare socks and a thin blazer over a buttoned shirt, over a wool undershirt. No scarf, no hat, no gloves. The pass worked like a wind tunnel blasting everyone who went through. The donkey refused to continue on the return leg of the trip. It brayed and stayed in one spot, stalled them there for over an hour, while my father yanked the collar again and again, trying to get them both home.

In both dreamscapes, he would think, "How can this be? I thought this ordeal ended a long time ago. I thought I was finished with the miserable part of my life."

Fifteen years before their divorce, I dreamt I was stranded in my parents' village at night. I stood outside on a rock-tiled road in the rain, looking into brightly decorated North American shop windows; faceless white mannequins, as attractive and becoming as plastic coat-hangers, were draped in pastel clothes. Fluorescent light spilled out of the stores; neon lights from shop signs glared off the wet pavement stones. The stores had replaced street-level spaces that used to house chickens, goats and mules.

Everything had changed, I thought. I'd never find what I needed.

In a blink, I stood at the entry to my father's childhood home atop a crooked, steep stairway, scared and alone—wondering where my parents were.

I knocked on the door: no answer.

I tried the handle, pushing against the wood with my shoulder in case the lock had rusted shut. I had no idea how to get in, or what was inside. No one had lived in the house for over twelve years.

An extended loop played: How could I let this happen? How could I let this happen? How could I let this happen? How could I let this happen? I can't stay here. I can't stay here. I can't stay here. This is not safe. This is not safe. Not safe. Not safe. Not safe.

I leaned my forehead against the door, unsure where to turn.

A man appeared at the foot of the stairs and made the gesture for 'there's nothing left,' his hand cocked like a pistol and pivoting his palm. "You won't get in without your mother. She has the key."

I couldn't see his face, couldn't make out if he was family or foe, or as with my mom's relatives, both. "But I'm not talking to my mother!"

"Boh." He shrugged, and threw both hands up. In the mental dialect dictionary I used to suss out conversations, "Boh" was in between "I don't know" and "I don't care." A daughter not speaking with her mother: poor woman, giving birth to such an ingrate.

"This isn't her house. It's my father's," I shouted. No reply. As conveniently as he appeared, he vanished, the winding roads empty in every direction I looked. I sat down on the steps, huddled against the wall and wished for a guide, someone who would explain everything.

I woke up wondering about the key.

I woke up and started recording my dreams in a diary.

By that point, my early twenties, I'd been looking for answers for a decade. Searching for reasons with the help of first a psychiatrist and then a therapist. The first of many attempts to solve a problem that had no solution.

In the fictional world built by Gene Rodenberry into the enormously successful *Star Trek* franchise, cadets at Starfleet are put through their training paces with a test based on a no-win situation: the Kobayashi Maru. The only person to ever "pass" the test is Captain Kirk, and he cheated. Every Saturday morning when episodes of classic *Star Trek* aired, I sat on the couch, eyes fixed on the television, dearly wanting to believe in a future where peace was the singular option. My mother would watch with me when she'd finished prepping salad and rapini for lunch. She liked Kirk, and I loved Spock, the Vulcan who favoured reason over rage. Played by Leonard Nimoy, Spock often remarked on humans as unruly, irrational and illogical beings.

Every day, my parents proved him right.

THE LOVERS.

The Lovers
(VI)

*She muses on the sacred role
of fate — affairs of future souls
depend on decisions made at the
intersection of chance and choice.*

Nonno Gennaro suggested the marriage between his son, thirty-year-old Michelantonio, and my mother-to-be, eighteen-year-old Lucia. My mother's family was in favour of the match; they wanted to offload their troubled daughter. She had brought scandal onto the clan by cavorting with a group of zingari and nearly running off with one when she was seventeen.

My father had been living in Canada for three years, working in a meat factory, saving money, learning to drive and strolling through Toronto's Little Italy at night. He hung out in billiard bars and played Scopa for candy. He drank wine and espresso and drove to Niagara Falls every chance he could. He got up early in the mornings without an alarm and went to work as a butcher in a building instead of tilling a field or coaxing a donkey uphill.

Thirty and unmarried, in 1965 Italy, people must have crossed themselves when my father walked by. "Whatever that guy has, O Dio, don't let anyone in my family catch it. Give it to my neighbour, the brute."

Thirty was much too old to be single. Canadian living showered him with comfort and cash, but no wife, no life—the classic unspoken motto of his background meant wedding bells had to sound soon. He'd returned to Bonefro for a three-month visit, and in his dwindling days, anxious mothers paraded two teenagers across his path. He didn't fancy either of them. Too young: the generation gap in rural Italy could mean the difference between a feast or famine childhood, the opportunity for an education or illiteracy.

My grandfather stepped up the pressure. As the son, custom demanded that my father produce an heir. My mother came from a wealthy family. Her father was nicknamed the Baron, based on an apocryphal tale that a villager saw him counting all his money in the window one day—making sure everyone could see how well off he was. As if anyone courted envy in a place like Molise where everyone needed to dodge malocchio.

Dad finally bowed to familial pressure and picked one, so my grandmother went to visit her cousin, my mother's father.

This gets complicated, I know.

Trust me: after tasked with making a family tree in fifth grade, the one Nonno helped fill in, I created multiple flow charts of all my relatives to understand the many connections myself. Essentially, my folks were already blood before a branch was grafted back onto the same oak. The villagers considered the union a good match because my mother's side had money.

)

I assume my maternal grandparents greeted my father's parents with wine, salami, provolone and the muted cheer that passed for joyful countenance in people with hardened dispositions. My father says, "They put something in my caffè." Nevertheless, the scheduled marriage ceremony would occur four weeks before the end of my father's trip.

On a clear-sky morning in March, he walked with his mother to his fiancée's home where they collected a procession of paesani and relatives to continue on to Santa Maria Delle Rose Church. My grandmothers, Femia and Sapooch, retreated to prepare the post-ceremony feast. Given what I know now, that must have been terrible for the former, and possibly an opportunity for the latter to plant the seeds of poison that would eventually kill Femia.

So the story goes.

On their honeymoon in Campobasso, the capital of mountainous Molise, Carabinieri—a member of the Italian military police—pulled them over. He asked for my father's autograph, convinced he'd netted the singing sensation Bobby Solo and my mother was a soon-to-be-famous starlet. My father insisted he wasn't the famous crooner. The officer remained doubtful as he studied my dad's chiselled features and scanned the casual glamour of my mom's flawless complexion and wavy chestnut locks.

From Bonefro, my father took my mother on the path that he and many other Molisans had followed. They made their way back to Canada, where the streets were paved with asphalt.

They landed together in Toronto in April 1968, and moved into my Aunt Angelina's duplex. Four families had lived there together when my father first relocated to Toronto: Aunt Angie, her husband and their two boys; my father's older married sister, Sofia, her husband and their two boys; my dad, who slept on a cot in the kitchen; and another family who rented the top floor of the tiny home. The folks upstairs left, and the dwelling remained decidedly less crowded with six adults and four kids.

I appeared, swaddled in pink, before their first anniversary: the only girl in the family, the only daughter of the only son. No matter how often I asked, no brother or sister followed.

Nonno Gennaro voiced his displeasure at the end of his family line. "That's it for us then," he would lament to anyone who'd listen. He grieved and said so long to the dynasty with no dominion. "The Fantettis are finished."

My father told him to shut his blabbering mouth.

There are hundreds of ways to invite misfortune, and talk reigned as one of the easiest.

At home, I pestered both parents to tell me a story. My mother knew a few doozies she could recite with flourish. I'd sit at the kitchen table, legs swinging, eating my favourite lunch of diced tomatoes mixed with beaten egg batter, a delicious dish I could eat with my hands. Ripped slices of crusty round bread were used as spoons. I'd scoop the warm sauce directly from the bowl in the middle of the table while offering suggestions: "Tell me the one about the cats who ran the kingdom again. Or the one about the good girl and her bad sister who grew a donkey tail on her forehead."

Or the one my mother preferred:

"A woodcutter marries a woman from a village nearby—a woman he hardly knows. She is a stranger to him, but she is beautiful and quiet. The woodcutter is not a man of many words. He wants a silent wife. A month after the wedding, everything seems settled for the newlyweds; they are content. The woodcutter always goes to bed before his wife because he has to get up early to chop wood. She stays up late cleaning the hearth, mending his clothes, washing and drying the dishes—doing the chores a good woman must do."

The characters in my mother's tales would always pause to offer an aside on what it took to be a respectable woman and a good wife. Sometimes, lost in a forest at night, a peasant girl with the heart of a princess would muse that no one would want her if she couldn't keep a tidy home, sew a button on a shirt or embroider a tablecloth.

"One morning the woodcutter goes out with his axe to fell more trees and gather firewood for the oncoming winter. There's a chill in the air as he sets out from his little cottage. While he's out in the forest, he's attacked by an enormous grey wolf. The woodcutter manages to cut off one of the wolf's front paws. The wolf retreats, running off, disappearing into the forest."

"How can he run without a paw?"

"The wolf manages to run off limping and crying."

"Howling. Wolves can't cry."

"Do you want me to finish? The wolf runs away. The woodcutter retrieves the paw, wraps it in burlap cloth and throws it into his sack. The injured woodcutter hurries back to his cottage. He finds his wife sitting by the fire, preparing his lunch. He doesn't want to scare her, so he doesn't tell her what happened. Better she doesn't know there's a wolf nearby. She thinks he should lie down, but the man sits at the table, shaken and visibly upset. His wife asks why he's home so early in the day. He tells her he had an accident. You need to be careful, says the young wife. She puts his lunch in front of him—and the woodcutter notices his wife's left hand is wrapped in a dirty dish towel, a mappina.

"He asks, 'What happened to you?' and she answers, 'I burned my hand this morning,' but this upsets the woodcutter. No one wants a clumsy woman in the kitchen. She goes back to stoking the fire, turning her back to him. The woodcutter reaches into his bag and pulls out the cloth. He unwraps it and finds a human hand where he expected to see a wolf paw. He shouts and drops the hand on the table. His wife whirls around, her face all white. He looks closer at the hand. It's a female hand. Then he notices the wedding band on the ring finger: he recognises the band.

"His wife says nothing. She tends the embers, keeping her burned hand hidden. He reaches for her arm and pulls off the dish towel, sees instantly that she is missing her hand. He grabs his axe and strikes her dead with one blow.

"People," Mamma would end with conviction, "are not who you think they are, so you have to be careful."

I wore my father down with a repeated request for a story. He maintained he knew one outside of *Aesop's Fables*.

"A young woman wants to marry, and she has two young men interested in her. She likes both men. She needs to find a way to make a decision. She tells both men she's going on a trip and to meet her at the airport to say goodbye. One guy comes dressed in a nice suit. Showered, clean, nice aftershave. Looks very nice. The second man came straight from work. He was in his mechanic's uniform, with dirt and oil from engine on his pants. Which man she should marry?"

"The man in the suit."

"No. Pay attention. He doesn't have a job." My dad shook his head. "That's why he has time to prepare his 'so long, see you later,' he doesn't have anything else to do."

No castles. No felines with the gift of gab. No wizened old women asking for a drink of water at a well, ready to bestow treasures for a simple show of compassion.

"That's not a story. That's a puzzle for an awful situation. Where did you hear that?"

"You asked for story, I told you a story. If you don't like, you don't like. Nothing I can do."

THE CHARIOT.

The Chariot
(VII)

She travels to the source and considers the power of bitter roots.

W hen I was eleven, we packed our bags for Bonefro again. My father, fed up and hell-bent on finding an antidote for my mother's ongoing nasty streak and fatiguing delusions, wanted his in-laws, the Colombos, to talk sense into their daughter. He thought Italy could provide a remedy, or perhaps medical help, at the insistence of family. The village, without the buffer of my beloved grandmother, was the loneliest place on Earth. I was an outsider, almost an outcast.

Nonno Gennaro had decamped six months before, bored beyond measure in Canada. He missed the natural splendour of the village. Even my reunion with him couldn't lessen my sorrow. The summer sun, the southern heat, the patchwork olive and jade greens of the surrounding land—I wished to experience it all with Femia.

Across from the house lived fourteen-year-old twins who befriended me. Their friendship meant putting up with harsh criticism and light bullying. Nicknamed *L'Americana*, I accepted my status as a target. Openly mocked for my accent, my comfortable Canadian existence without farm chores and my hair, recently chopped by mother into a hideous bob: my everything. One night, I stepped out onto the balcony off the upstairs room to gawk at the star-filled sky. Hundreds twinkled against the midnight blue curtain, a breathtaking sight for a kid from the suburb of a sizable metropolis. The next day, the twins told everyone about spotting me in my full-length nightgown, hanging out on the tiny ledge.

One girl jeered, "Were you looking for Romeo? This is no place for romantics, Juliet."

My mother's older sister, Gina, showed up from Belgium on this visit; the first time I met my maternal aunt. After the exchange of cheek kisses and pleasantries — "Femia's namesake resembles her so much" — she said, "Your mother was fine before she had you."

Throughout our Italian vacation, my mother's parents and siblings commented that Mamma had been absolutely fine before she'd left the village. In front of us, they debated the factors:

a) The move to another country and breathing in the crisp Canadian air

b) Marriage to my father, himself a descendant of that wasteful dad — Gennaro

c) Motherhood: babies are absurdly demanding; I must have been more taxing than most

d) All of the above contributed to her psychotic break

They insisted we treat my mother, the baby in the family, with maximal kindness, compassion and consideration—the three qualities she never expressed toward us.

I accepted the Colombos' mixed up memories as truth. I believed I could never have children or bedlam would ensue. I internalized every comment as if it were a fact. And I wanted nothing to do with these people.

A spectacular disaster awaited us at the first appointment with an Italian specialist.

Recommended by someone who knew someone who knew someone who'd heard of someone else's troubled wife, another poor soul who found the transition from village life to urban living a trial, the doctor-slash-mayor of Campomarino—a small town forty kilometres northeast of Bonefro—assured my dad that he'd cured many women of hysteria. He exuded the arrogance of a man who bathed daily in the cheap, pungent cologne of his own self-importance.

When mom declined to enter the medical office that doubled as headquarters for civic planning, Nonna Sapooch attacked. She shoved her daughter against an exterior rock wall in the open courtyard and wrapped both hands around mom's neck. Sapooch pressed her thumbs into my mother's throat and squeezed, cutting off air. Sapooch choked her in full view of the street and passersby.

A mini-riot ensued.

Mom wriggled like an insect pinned to a board. She clawed at Sapooch's fingers, her face turning a ghostly white tinged with blue.

Dad shouted, "Ma che cazzo—lascia, lasciala—" He leapt to his feet, forcibly restraining his mother-in-law, pulling her back and holding one arm behind her while she struggled to slap and kick her daughter. "Mannagia—la stai soffocando, fermeti—"

I pulled on Sapooch's other arm. "Mammanon, no! Ferma—" I tugged at the fabric of her sleeve. She flailed to dislodge me and shake off my father. I tumbled backward, scraping palms to catch my fall.

Nonno Baron made a pathetic attempt to control his wife. "Now, now. Let's not make a fuss." He stood to the side, one hand patting Sapooch's shoulder as she wrestled to get at my mother.

In the midst of the melee, one clear thought rang through me, pealing like the church bells of Bonefro: we were doomed.

Sapooch swore to kill my mother if she didn't stop destroying their family's good reputation with outrageous behaviour.

"Good reputation? She's crazy like her mother and her grandmother before her," my father said.

Sapooch loosened her grip. She whirled around to face off with him. "What?"

Mom bent over; hacking and gulping for air, she rubbed her throat. Pink stripes the shape of my grandmother's fingers curled around her neck.

I rocked on my heels, and then moved away to the farthest corner of the courtyard, witness to the legacy of a vicious temper.

The doctor quickly ushered my parents into his office to interview them. I edged away from my grandparents as we waited for my folks to return. The doctor prescribed a sedative for my mother.

"What about treatment for him?" Sapooch thrust her thumb at my father. "What if there's something wrong with him?"

Dad threw his hands up in frustration. "Gesù Cristo—"

"No, Signora. He's not the problem."

A nervous laugh escaped me, and I spoke in English, "Holy cow, like that's not obvious to anybody with eyeballs in their head."

Sapooch scowled. "What did you say? Say it again. Say it so I can understand you."

"Nothing."

Dad moved between us. "Let's take the prescription to the pharmacy. It can be filled while we eat lunch."

I hung close, bumping into him as we walked to avoid my grandmother's stony-faced glare.

Back in Bonefro, we parted company with Sapooch and the Baron near the piazza and made our way home uphill along the cobbled road of Via Rosello, where, in late afternoon, the row of linked houses offered shade from the June sun. Nonno Gennaro waved at me when we came into view. He sat by the balcony door in the seat Femia used to occupy.

My mother took her first dose and went upstairs for a nap. "Allora? Che te ditte u dottore?"

"He prescribed a sedative. We'll see if it works, or we'll go back."

Nonno put out his cigarette and scratched his chest. "Watch the moon. Both of you. Pay attention to the phases of the moon, and stay out of her way when it's full."

A warning. An attempt to predict my mother's lapses into lunacy by tracking the orbit of Earth's satellite. Ancient advice: a step above reading goat entrails.

Down the narrow road in front of my grandmother's house lived an old woman named Carmella who spoke in garbled speech. Her skin was wrinkled tree bark with intersecting lines woven across her forehead and cheeks. I tried not to stare at her gaping mouth. One part of her face had been paralyzed when she was five, and never healed properly, so that she could never fully close her lips. The top of her mouth was caved in, as with people missing all their top teeth. When she first walked up to greet me, the top of her body swayed slightly side to side like a metronome as she limped over.

She bent to examine me closely. I reached for her hand, clasped it and greeted her with two kisses, one on each cheek.

Her lips, covered in spittle, quivered. She brushed her eyes with the back of her hand, like a child might to stop tears. She uttered a series of vowel sounds with no glottal stops. I turned to my dad.

"She thinks you look exactly like your grandmother did at your age. She says you're nice like your Nonna Femia. She was born the same year, they grew up together, and she misses your grandmother."

The next day, while I sat near the French doors of the balcony in my grandmother's old chair, I heard the twins yelling. I looked out to see them shouting at Carmella, right behind her. Amalia gesticulated rudely that Carmella should make herself scarce; she looked like she might shove the senior. Anna Maria spat at Carmella's feet.

I ran down the stairs and put myself between the twins and Carmella. "What are you doing? Are you crazy? Leave her alone."

"This is none of your concern, Americana. Go back where you came from." Anna Maria scowled.

"She's an old lady. Stop it."

"She's a thief. She steals eggs from our chicken."

"Maybe she's hungry. What is the matter with you?"

"Maybe she's hungry," mimicked Amalia. "L'Americana thinks she knows hunger."

Anna Maria and Amalia's mother appeared on their stoop. "Eufemia, fatti fatte tuoi. Mind your own business. This doesn't concern you at all." The twins' mother scolded Carmella, shouting that the old hag was asking for a beating.

I stood on the road in the heat of the noonday sun and stared, open mouthed.

Anna Maria snickered. "Close your mouth before you give mosquitos a new home. Before you end up with the same problem."

When I think of that day, even all these days into the future, I can still feel the sun on my face, the tingling burn that seeped through the layers of my skin. And the yearning that churned from a dark corner inside me, reaching through my ribs, circling my heart, a swirling shame that I couldn't protect Carmella. I couldn't protect my dad. I couldn't save anyone.

I pulled out the unique tool I had to make the girls feel inept. I spoke English, clipping my consonants with the smugness of someone who knew her second language offered a host of opportunities. "The sooner we leave this stupid place, the better." I turned back to the house.

I threw myself into the role of the Good Samaritan, calling a greeting to Carmella morning, noon and night.

Carmella continued to slobber speech that I couldn't make out. Until one day, when I stood playing alone with a bouncy ball against the front wall of the house. She lurched toward me, and I stopped, concentrated on her sounds.

She pointed to my rainbow halter top and velour lavender shorts. "Cover yourself up. You're dressed like a *putana*."

Excited, I ran inside to tell my father I'd understood the

woman everyone called the Mute, realising mid-stride that she'd called me a whore.

My dad laughed. "Don't be upset, Chickpea. She's had a hard life."

The night before our scheduled return to Toronto, the house filled with cousins coming to say goodbye. My father's suitcase lay packed and ready. The one I shared with my mother hadn't been touched.

"I'm going upstairs to pack," I announced to everyone around me.

My father grabbed my wrist and pulled me to his side. "You're not coming. You and your mom are staying here a little longer."

"Che? Ma per che?" My tongue was having trouble forming anything longer than one syllable in Italian, the signals from my brain getting stuck. I trembled. My hands shook. I yanked my arm out of his grasp, almost pulling him from his seat. "No, no, no. No! No way I'm staying here."

I looked over at my mother. She stared at the wall with her head bobbing drowsily. On meds, her movements simulated those of a zombie: she knew. Nonno Gennaro avoided eye contact: he knew. The other guests, they knew.

I turned back to face my dad and hit him full force across his chest. "No!"

He grabbed my arms and held them at my sides. "Don't make like a crybaby in front of everybody. Ti de sta qua. You have to stay. Your mother needs to be here and keep taking medicine."

"That's not my fault. Let her stay. Let her live here. She loves it here."

His expression hardened; his lips flattened like they would right before he'd yell at my mother.

I ran upstairs and hid behind my cot. Six more weeks of summer. Six more weeks of the twins. Six more weeks of the bullying that passed for teasing in a rural poverty-stricken place. Six weeks of being alone with my mother. I chewed the inside of my mouth, clenched my jaw until it ached. Downstairs, the party of goodbyes continued. I tried to block out the sound of boisterous voices punctuated with raucous laughter by covering my ears.

My dad didn't come upstairs, didn't come looking for me.

I was devastated. After an hour, I reached into my purse, took markers and a notepad. I drew a rose and wrote my father a note: *Dad, don't worry. I'll look after mom.*

I stuck the slip underneath his shirts. What I wanted to write was: *Please come back. Don't leave me here.*

I lay down on the cot and prayed that when I woke in the morning, this would have been a bad dream. That I would go to the airport in Rome and travel to my real home in Toronto—the city where I could wear whatever I wanted. The city where no one knew me or my family—where the bandits, the fake barons, meant nothing. The city where I could get lost in a crowd rather than be watched, judged and deemed unworthy.

Mom and I stayed put even though her parents argued we needed to move in with them. I refused, and my mother made a show of pleading with me in front of her brother. She didn't want to stay with her folks either, but she wouldn't own up to it and shifted the blame to me. My grandparents and uncle countered that I was a selfish spoiled brat. As if my mother could ever be convinced to do anything other than exactly what she wanted. I heard her lie to her parents and make me the culprit.

"Meh tu pense che i' nen'de capisce?" Astonished at her attempted deception, I interrupted her incriminating monologue. I would have called her a liar except I had no allies.

She pinched my arm and hurried us back to the house.

We ate all our meals with my mother's parents. A day after my dad left, my mother stopped taking the meds that slowed her rages and made her sluggish, but she hadn't pummeled me, and instead she seemed delighted to bask in the careful attention of her own bitter, malicious mother.

Nonna Sapooch had groomed her youngest daughter to be a brutish gossipmonger. They shared a love of shredding women through sarcasm and barbed comments. I avoided drawing attention to myself as much as possible, in order to live with the fragile peace.

On the morning that the three of us—mom, Nonna Sapooch and I—took the bus to see the specialist near Termoli one last time, my mother and I walked out into the Adriatic at low tide. Above us the clouds rippled in a mackerel sky. I gasped; the Italian countryside dazzled—a museum painting come to life, but I'd been too overwhelmed to appreciate the beauty, distracted by the ornery undercurrent that ran like electricity through my mother and grandmother.

While my mom and Sapooch visited the doctor, I waited alone on the sizzling beach for what felt like hours, hot and thirsty, sitting hunched over to make myself invisible. A man older than my father ambled by and tried to engage me in conversation. Then another offered to buy ice cream. Sweat formed on my scalp, dribbled down my sides and pooled on my back. I ignored the men and stared at the horizon, steadily sifting sand through my fingers, ready to grab a fistful if anyone lingered too long.

"Come on. We're leaving." Sapooch appeared at the edge of my towel, dressed all in black, from stockings to her headkerchief, out of place among the bikini crowd. She shifted her weight from foot to foot, resembling a pudgy crow scavenging for scraps.

With sweaty armpits, my skin slick from fear and heat, I wiped the sand off my legs and scrambled to my feet.

I fell into step beside my mom as we trekked back to the bus terminal. "What did the doctor say?"

Sapooch swatted my backside. "She doesn't need a doctor. There's nothing wrong with her."

That night, I dreamt we missed our flight, and I was doomed to dwell in Bonefro forever.

Four weeks later, my mother and I made our way through Canada Customs. The agent flagged us as a problem. My mother would have to pay duty on all the gold jewellery she had bought in Italy. In under a week, she had spent on pricey baubles all the money my father had left with her. The agent told me to go through the gate and return with my dad so he could pay the fine. I stepped through the sliding doors in Arrivals and heard my father shouting my name.

"O Dio! What happened? What's happened to you?" My father measured my upper arm by squeezing index finger and thumb like a blood pressure test. "Didn't they feed you?"

My appetite left and barely resurfaced that summer: I'd lost twelve pounds in six weeks. I hadn't noticed until I put on my jeans for the plane ride home and had to keep tugging them up.

I shrugged, and led him back to my mother and the agent. Before my mother could say anything, my dad grabbed her by the throat.

The agent yelled for security while my mom clawed at his

hands and wheezed.

I screamed and pulled on his shirt.

He shook me off. "Did you remember to feed her? Why is she a skeleton? What kind of a mother doesn't provide for her own child?" He tugged on the gold necklace. Evidence of the money she'd blown. "You're a disgrace—a beast I should have left behind in Bonefro."

Two guards ran over. One held his palms up as he approached us. In a loud, firm voice, he chastised my dad, "Sir, you have to calm down. Calm down." The other spoke into a crackling walkie-talkie.

I screamed again. "Ne ge niende, Papa! Niende." It's nothing. Nothing.

He let go and grasped my forearm again. His voice broke, "Ti si perse tropp sai pese."

"Is everything going to be okay here, sir? Are you going to control yourself?"

I begged the men to leave us alone. "It's not his fault. He's upset." I pointed to my waistline and held out the jeans. "It's me. My fault. I didn't eat enough. I lost weight. He's an Italian dad. He thinks I should always be eating."

The guards exchanged glances while I held my breath.

My mother cleared her throat and coughed. She looked from my father to me. I could see the distortion in her features again, pinched mouth, scrunched forehead and that unmerciful gaze with the glimmer of defiance in her eyes. A noxious mix of envy and entitlement. She was like the mad scientist from a low-grade sci-fi film—constantly performing experiments on us, unfailing in her research and also the tireless catalyst. She'd found a way to make my father pay for the necklace more than once. She'd figure out how to punish me for the ruckus.

Strength
(VIII)

She requires fortitude
and self-preservation.

November in Alderwood, our south Etobicoke neighbourhood overwhelmed with charcoal grey. The cinderblock-coloured sky matched the cement sidewalks. The horizon disappeared, and we floated against a backdrop of drab and dreary, a spatial distortion that made it difficult to distinguish up from down.

My parents, in the suburban language of the 1980s, hated each other's guts. Late into the night, they bickered, and I begged them both to stop.

"Can't you hear your own daughter asking you to be quiet?"

"Tell me who you were with today. Was it that whore Giuseppina? What motive would you have for chasing another woman? With me waiting at home, making your dinner, you chase the tail of a fat old bitch."

"You're insane. I work hard to put food on the table and keep the roof over the head of crazy woman. And this is the thanks I get. Not even the chance to rest my head in my own home.

"You want gratitude? I'll show you and your slut gratitude. You start with me and I'll finish you. Understand me? I'll finish you. Don't worry about me. I'll be a widow before I ever come close to getting divorced."

"There's no talking reason to you. You're impossible."

My mother's temper would propel her out of bed at night. She vented by slamming all the cupboards and doors, breaking through the plaster to release the people she heard living in the walls.

In the mornings, my father would inspect the damage and grumble to himself. "This is no life for a human being. This is no life."

The first time she broke all the mirrors in the upstairs bathroom, we had no warning. A screech jolted me out of bed. My heart lurched with panic. The wall on the other side of my bed shook as my mother repeatedly slammed the metre-long, mirrored medicine cabinet until the glass shattered and sprinkled the floor with jagged pieces.

"Ma che fai? Che ti pozzone chiede—" Dad waved me back to bed. "Leave her. Don't go near her right now."

In silhouette, I couldn't make out her distorted features, but I knew them well enough to picture: a contorted mouth, flared nostrils and flinty eyes. I pulled the blankets over my head and prayed she wouldn't kill us while we slept.

He replaced the mirrors dozens of times—if the seven years of bad luck was true, it would take lifetimes for my mother to pay off the debt incurred to misfortune. Then he gave up and went for the quick fix. I put on makeup using a giant shard adhered to the wall with crazy glue.

I was thirteen, my mother thirty-three, my father forty-four, and we were all miserable. After a Sunday that had yawned and spit out an afternoon of bowling on television, we visited my Aunt Angelina and Uncle Mauro in Mississauga. On the Gardiner Expressway, my father sped along within the speed limit while cars droned past as if they were participating in the Indy 500. My mother muttered under her breath, accusing my father of having multiple affairs.

"But why? Tell me why you did it?" she asked over and over.

My father caught my eye in the rearview mirror, we were both in the habit of ignoring my mother's words, but trained to listen for a change in pitch, in timber, a signal switch in tone that acted as the warning bell. He let out a tired sigh. "Are you crazy? Or trying to drive me crazy?"

"He's right. Ma, please, give it a rest."

My mother half turned in her seat to face me. "Who was talking to you, sporcaccione? Fate i cazzi tuoi. This doesn't concern you. Zingara." She gave me her Medusa look, the one that could freeze water in an instant. The look usually left my father so stupefied I believed she could turn all men into stone. Her eyes acted as a sensor alarm for me, but I failed to notice in time.

She leaned sideways then lunged forward, grabbed the steering wheel and yanked hard. Our car swerved into the next lane. I screamed. My father swore as he fought to regain control of the vehicle. We were the road traffic sign in action: a slippery car warning for everyone else on the highway, leaving a trail of wavy lines as my dad scuffled for the steering wheel. Horns blared from angry commuters.

My mother let go and laughed. Not a maniacal shriek of amusement, not the cackle she could let out. She guffawed like a person who'd heard a brilliant joke.

If anyone in the cars whizzing past had looked out a side window, they would have seen me bent over, hands protecting my head, braced for impact.

Years later in yoga class, lying stretched out on a mat after a vigorous class, I realised I'd been holding the same pose for years—whether I went for a walk, sat for a meal or lounged on a couch watching television—my spine curved with fear. Even when I slept, my body curled on one side, hands tucked under my chin, half fetal and half fearful—forever seeking calm and attempting to rest in the crash position.

The following November, another wintry morning during grade nine, my high school debut, I sat on our. top step lacing up my running shoes. The Evans Avenue bus left every half hour.

My mother shouted, "Wait—" she climbed the stairs, wiped her hands on her apron and removed it. She fixated on my notebooks, and frowned. That gorgon gaze again, the red sky at morning stare.

"I'm driving you to school today."

I balked. "Dad left you the car?"

"I'm going to pick it up now from your father. Then I'm driving you to school." In the mirror behind the closet door, she primped her hair off her forehead and smoothed down the sides.

"But you'll make me late before you even get there."

I studied her face. This day would unfurl into madness.

She swapped her house slippers for pumps and put on her coat. "When I tell you to wait, you wait. You do what I say, and you do everything I say. Understand?"

She slammed the door shut behind her and locked the bolt. Insult to the injury that was surely coming.

I sat still and cursed my lack of courage, frustrated that I couldn't will myself to get up and leave. Maybe when I came home she'd have forgotten. But more likely she would drive to my high school and search the hallways until she found me. Then she'd drag me out the front entrance by my hair.

In middle school, she had once come up behind me and had attacked me in front of a group of gape-mouthed girls, and the memory was still fresh. She towed me backwards while a boy standing with us yelled, "Hey—you can't do that." He turned to the others, "She can't do that. That's abuse."

I held up my hand to stop him from helping, from interfering. "Don't. It will be worse if I don't give in." I usually capitulated. Nothing could tame her Category Five fury—no seeking shelter, waiting for the storm to subside and hoping the house didn't cave in. As my world expanded, farther from her scope of control, she amped up her frustration.

That damp morning, so foggy and overcast, I wanted to disappear into the heavy mist outside and never return. I wondered where I could go that she wouldn't find me. Where could I hide? What would happen to my father? I sat and listened to the clock pendulum swaying, the minute hand ticking until it struck eight o'clock. The wind-up whir, the constant clicking noise. I hated that grandfather clock, a wedding gift to my mother from her godparents.

By 8:30 I thought I would do it, I would go. I sat and chewed my fingernails and the fleshy part of my thumb. At 8:45 I heard the car pull up in the driveway. I ran outside.

"Do you even know where to go?"

"State zitte. Get in."

We stayed silent for the brief ten-minute drive. I fumed and hoped she'd stay on the correct side of the yellow dotted line. She'd learned to drive when I was six: at a bend in the road on

Horner Avenue beyond Mimico Correctional Centre, she drove us toward oncoming traffic. I cringed and reached for the dashboard, too small to make contact. She swatted my arms down. I squirmed and turned sideways in my seat to avoid the head-on collision. Shocked drivers blared their horns and skidded out of the way. Cars pulled over to the side of the road, and startled men exited their vehicles to shout at my mother as we whipped past.

She pulled into the high-school parking lot, and I slinked out without saying a word. I signed in late at the front office and slid quietly into history class.

On her way home, she rear-ended a truck stopped at a red light at Kipling and Evans Avenues, less than a kilometre away from the factory where my dad worked.

That night we ate dinner in silence. I sat with my Archie comic in front of my plate, a habit that annoyed both my parents. I pointed out that since they rarely spoke at the table except to argue, I could read instead of being asked to referee the battle. The comics worked as a barrier, a screen that shielded me from observing my mother, who allowed tomato sauce to drip down her chin onto the tablecloth or her plate. She never wiped her face.

Once my father called the spectacle disgusting. For weeks after, my mother stood and ate from a pot over the sink. When she returned to the table, she doubled down on her atrocious manners, stuffing her face until her cheeks bulged like a chipmunk's, speaking with a full mouth and speckling our food with her wet crumbs. I'd endured having my face cleaned by her spit in a handkerchief, and she wouldn't touch a napkin until she was finished shovelling food into her mouth.

After another meal of greasy eggplant and burnt ground

beef, my father announced that he would go for an espresso. Within minutes of stepping outside, he rushed back.

"Lucie!" He bellowed from the side door. "What the hell happened to the car?"

I put down my reading material. "What happened?"

"What business is it of yours?" To my father, she called, "What? What's the matter?"

"What's the matter? The car is smashed. What's the matter—you think I'm an idiot. Come out here and tell me what happened. Don't make me come to you or you'll regret it when I call the police and tell them to take you to jail. Come see what you did."

I gathered my comics and went to my room.

I heard my father shouting from the garage. He came back inside and asked me to join him at the upstairs dining table. Charged with the role of mediator, marriage counsellor and quasi-wife, I ended up as the sounding board for all my father's questions and concerns. My mother held zero interest in solving any household problems, balancing a budget or maintaining the vegetable garden. Adult conversations occurred without her input. Guidance duty exhausted me: I felt old and weary, never wise. Exasperated, I trudged down the hall.

Ignoring my father's agitated state, Mom offered to make us all espressos. She insisted that she had bumped the front fender on re-entering the garage. She referred to the damage—the metal crunched and fanned like an accordion—as a scratch. A scrape that would cost over a thousand dollars at an auto body repair shop.

My father removed his glasses and rubbed his eyes. "I don't know what now. We should be call the police?"

"Yes. We should."

"Why? It's a scratch."

"We have to call them and report there's been an accident."

"You're a snake—"

"Fine. And you're a terrible driver."

"You'd call your daughter a snake? You, a beast born to destroy and cause ruin—do you have venom coursing through your veins instead of blood?"

"Papa, don't—" The last time he had defended me (and then left to hang out at the billiard club), she had punched me in the ribs so hard I sported a bruise the size of a saucer.

My mother left in a huff to evening Mass at St. Ambrose. Perhaps she could petition the patron saint of automobile accidents.

My father shouted after her, "Now you pray? Look at this," my father jerked his chin at her retreating figure. "The devil wants to attend church. Unbelievable. I don't know what to do with her. We should call the police and make the report."

I stood up, walked over to the rotary dial on the wall and called 9-1-1.

The officers arrived within twenty minutes. They had been looking for my mother since morning. She had struck a truck on her route home after dropping me off at school. The driver crossed the intersection and pulled over to the side of the road to wait for my mother, but she drove on past. In the fog, the trucker couldn't make out the license plate details.

One of the officers, heavy-set with a handlebar moustache, questioned my father about the time of the accident, making it sound as though we had purposely been trying to hide the car.

"Why did it take you so long to call us, Mr. Fantet?"

"It's Fantetti," I corrected. A tight constricted sensation clutched my chest. It wasn't right, my father being treated poorly, being treated like a liar, a suspect. I wanted to tell the officer that he didn't know who he was dealing with. My deeply religious dad and Mr. moral compass, always the first to lend a hand. He lived and acted according to his preferred philosophy that we were all put here on Earth to help each other. My father was disgusted by cheaters and con artists, by men like his brother-in-law who bilked the government out of every penny he could.

What kind of detective ability did this officer have? Couldn't he see the man who sat before him? A man who had nothing but praise for his adopted country; a socialist in Canada, a communist in Italy, a citizen passionate about politics who had never missed voting in elections at any level of government. A man who didn't have to think about doing the right thing because no other option ever occurred to him.

He was the highest-paid butcher at his company and still laboured diligently to bring in the union. He was the shop steward until he took on bigger responsibilities in the company, an amiable man whom people loved. At the factory, they said, "If you can't get along with Mike, you can't get along with anybody." My father got along with everyone except my mother. The officer's tone suggested my father was a mobster attempting to dupe the local sheriff.

"Yes, yes, you right. You right. I should be call before. I was finding out after I coming home, maybe two hours before now."

"That's not an explanation, sir."

"No, no. You right, you right."

"How is that not an explanation? He didn't know. Then he did. When he did, we called you and now you know too."

"Eufemia," my father's forehead furrowed. In Italian he said, "Don't get upset. Don't get angry."

The second officer, the younger one, piped up, "Why didn't you report this earlier sir?"

"Are you for real? I told you why—you found out right after we did."

"Chickpea—is okay." He turned to the officers, "My wife, she makes trouble, but my daughter is difference. She likes to help. She's a good girl."

The officers explained they would be filing another report, and offered a mini lecture on the law and how the legal system could penalize hit-and-runs, how fortunate it was that my mother had not hurt or injured anyone.

"Yes, thanks God." My father nodded. "Thanks God."

"You should have called us sooner," the second officer repeated.

"Okay! We get it. We're late. So now what? Tell us, so now, what?" My jaw clenched and unclenched as I over-enunciated every word. A nerve ending pulsated behind my right ear, and my face warmed with shame. I stared at the officers, dared them to use the "Let me explain this to you simple-like" tone that they had used with my dad. As if he was stupid. As if he wasn't answering their questions as clearly as he could. As if his accented English was an alien language spoken in another galaxy.

My father unclasped his hands and raised his right inches off the table, palm down. He flapped his fingers slowly, and subtly shook his head. He wanted me to stay calm.

"No. I'm handling this, Dad. So now, what?"

The one with the bulging belly ignored me and spoke to Dad instead. "Where's your wife, sir?"

"She went to church. She be come home in a little bit. You want wait? I can take some food for you? My daughter can be make the coffee for you?"

"We'll come back later." Mr. Paunch took a final look around.

"Up to you. Is okay if you want to stay."

They left, sauntering out through the side door instead of making a spectacle at the front.

We said nothing to my mother when she came back from church. My father watched the grandfather clock, and I kept checking my wristwatch as it got later and later with no sign of the officers.

They returned at a quarter to midnight, three hours after we'd all gone to bed. I let the officers in while my mother got dressed in a housecoat. She offered her fresh-baked taralli biscuits. My father told her to stop offering nonsense dessert and insisted the officers try his homemade prosciutto. Within minutes, the table was covered with ricotta pie, soppresatta, a platter of Italian cheeses mixed with mortadella and capicollo and a bottle of homemade wine.

The officers put up a good fight but gave in when they realized my parents would not stop offering them food and drink, answering every question with "Please, you eat something, is good for you."

Every time one of the officers questioned my mother, she burst out laughing. "I no know." She shook her head coyly, shrugged and giggled. She was on her best behaviour, an act that didn't seem to convince the officers.

This second visit, they treated my father politely, with respect. Mr. Moustache observed my mother carefully while the other officer—the cute, clean-shaven, blue-eyed one who I could never forgive for coming back so late as to catch me in my pink flannel pyjamas—asked my parents different versions of the same questions. My father answered in a logical, sensible manner. Questions about when my mother arrived at his factory, how long she had been driving, when he first noticed the smashed front fender.

"Mrs. Fantetti, do you understand how serious this is? You can't leave the scene of an accident, ma'am." The older officer studied my mother's expressions, her body language. He rarely looked elsewhere.

My mother was under observation, and for once she chafed at the attention.

"Che ditte?" My mother threw herself into the part of misunderstood immigrant.

"Tu sai che ditte. S'acce che tu capische." I refused to participate in her charade. She understood everything the police asked her. My mother needed a buffer between psychosis and reality, not a translator.

Her soap opera antics were amateur theatre. "I no know. I no speaking good the English." In Italian she said, "You can't trust a man with a moustache." The final word she pronounced in English. She wanted to watch me scramble into peacemaker mode whenever she offended people or put me in an uncomfortable spot.

A look passed between the officers.

I faked a yawn. It was midnight on a school night. "She's admiring your moustache."

My mother scowled at me. Remembering she was in trouble, she brightened at the officers. "You want caffè? I make." She patted her hair, smoothing a wayward strand.

My father lowered his head, humiliated at hosting this audience of authority figures. "You see what I have to be live with?"

"Shut up, you stupid. I marry bad husband. No understand

nothing. I prepare espresso for everybody. Eufemia, take cups, bring from kitchen."

The older officer pushed back in his chair and stood. "No. No coffee. We have what we need to file the report. Mrs. Fantetti—"

"Lucy. My friend call me Lucy. Now we friendly."

"Mrs. Fantetti. You've had a driver's license for ten years. You should realize you committed a crime. People go to prison for what you did today."

I visualized my mother in the black-and-white striped uniform of a cartoon convict: a comforting thought. Perhaps the Almighty had finally heard my appeals for assistance.

"Mr. Fantetti, I suggest that you take your wife to see a doctor—a specialist—probably a psychiatrist. Her behaviour isn't normal for someone in her situation."

The younger officer nodded his agreement. Both looked stern.

Less than fifteen minutes in the same room as my mother, and both officers advise she see a psychiatrist. Fifteen minutes. I had been with her for almost fifteen years, and no one had ever made that suggestion before.

In the pause, I examined the lines of my palm. Not wanting to make eye contact with either of my parents, avoiding the police entirely, I pressed my thumbnail hard into a ridge, and grimaced.

"Thanks you. Very much. I'm sorry we meeting this way, but you was helping us very nice." My dad led the officers to the front door. I followed, watching them descend the veranda stairs. Snow fell in a swirling pattern with enormous snowflakes landing on the officers' uniforms and caps.

The night bore a bone-chilling cold that lingered. Winter

stormed on, bringing a record-breaking day of bitter cold in December and harsh storms that caused thousands of motorists to stall. Some days it seemed the sun would never break through the oppressive cloud carpet again.

Three weeks later, at an office in the Bloor West Village neighbourhood, a psychiatrist diagnosed my mother with paranoid schizophrenia.

The Hermit
(IX)

*She finds a guide who bears the
lamp of wisdom to illuminate the
path ahead.*

The schizophrenia diagnosis sent me into a spiral. I searched through my paperback dictionary and our set of encyclopedias for definitions that could help me decipher how to communicate with my mother. I read about Eugen Bleuler, the Swiss psychiatrist who coined the term when he treated famed ballet dancer Vaslav Nijinsky in 1919. Nijinsky had a nervous breakdown at thirty, never recovered and never danced again. Out of the list of possible symptoms I found—grandiose delusions, auditory hallucinations and paranoid beliefs of godly persecution—none described her expressionless gaze, or the delight she took in the suffering of others.

Even after her medical assessment, no one in the extended family knew what to make of my mother's erratic behaviour.

My Aunt Ida, my mother's sister-in-law, called from Montreal. "She should have another baby. That would focus her attention, and she wouldn't have time to throw these tantrums." Uncle Mauro, a man my father tolerated for Aunt Angelina's sake, suggested dad's leniency caused all the problems. "If you took off your belt and walloped her, she wouldn't fall out of line. She'd behave."

Everyone had an opinion they insisted on sharing with us, no matter how caveman or clueless their tips. Our dismal situation supplied two pastimes dear to southern Italians—gossiping and opining. We drifted in a sea of dreadful advice.

Old-world attitudes exported from the motherland: ground zero. All of the chaos so familiar. Molise, the pastoral region of big-hearted, loud-mouthed people who shouted at me—"She looks like her Nonna! She's so tall! Over here, come here and let me have a look at you!"—lived on as a place where objects in the memory were much closer than they appeared.

Dad drove me to my first appointment with Dr. Salima and sat in the waiting room. Dr. Salima was short; at 5'6", I towered over her. Her round face glowed a gorgeous caramel, the kind people in the 1980s tried to copy in tanning salons. With her auburn hair pulled back, she bore an uncanny resemblance to the actress who played the psychic in the movie *Poltergeist*. A good omen, I thought.

Her office was located in the same medical building on Bloor and Jane that my parents had gone to for my mother's psychiatric assessment from Dr. Amante. After a few follow up sessions with him, my mother's aggression, hostility and noncompliance put an end to the treatments.

In a fury over losing her driver's licence because of her diagnosis, she'd poured her Thorazine down the drain and pulverized the bathroom mirrors again. Arguments soared to atomic levels.

"Take your medicine, don't take your medicine, I don't care—I'm never letting you use the car again. You could kill somebody. You could ruin a life, and that means nothing to you." Dad turned to me mid-rant. "Can you believe this?"

I shrugged. "Sure. She's ruining our lives."

"That's right." He shouted down to the basement, where my mother was hanging the laundry and shrieking out a foul tirade. "Did you hear what your daughter said?"

"Pa no—"

"You're ruining our lives."

My mother paused her obscenity-strewn monologue. "I'll show you, gypsy. I'll show you."

"Thanks a lot, Papa. That's gonna cost me."

"I can't take any more. My nerves are broken. Me vade a prende nu caffè." He headed for the door.

"And now you're leaving? You're not serious? You're going to leave me with her like this?"

"I should stay here and be insulted in my own home? Go to your room and lock the door."

As a result of all this chaos and instability, I underwent a series of frightening and debilitating anxiety attacks.

"How can I help you?" Dr. Salima asked after I sat down.

I opened my mouth to speak and let out a muffled sob. A long, snot-ugly cry followed each time I tried to regain my composure. Not an unusual occurrence for my distraught 15-year-old self, but also not the first impression I wanted to make.

She handed me a box of tissues from her desk. She sat across from me, calm and quiet, waiting for me to finish.

I blew my nose several times before I could lift my head. The heavy weight of shame gripped me: embarrassment and despair pulsed through my body frequently enough that I thought the states of being could be tracked coursing through my veins.

She gave me an encouraging smile.

I imagined her banishing malevolent ghosts and sniffled an apology. "I don't know if I should be here. My mother probably should. She—she's very sick. She tried to kill me once when I was a kid. She believed I infiltrated and led a spy-prostitute ring." I bawled again as I told her about the diagnosis.

"That's a terrible illness. Hard on everyone. I'm sure it's been extremely confusing for you."

I nodded.

"Is that your father in the outer office? Why is he here?"

"I didn't know how to get here by myself." I'd developed a new tendency to panic anytime I went somewhere new. Timid and terrified all the time, exhausted from feigning normalcy, I adhered to my father like a baby duck—albeit the moody teenage version.

"I see." Dr. Salima stood and pointed out the window. "That's the subway station, right across the street. You sound brave. Maybe you need to practice independence. Next time, come without your father."

Bewildered by her compliment, I assured her of my cowardice. Bit by bit, I revealed the public panic attack that had spurred me to her office. Months before, I'd attended a special student-priced event at Roy Thompson Hall. An operetta, *The Merry Widow*. I arrived too early, and sat alone waiting for friends. A group of private school girls glowered at my outfit, a brown velour dress nearly a decade out of date, and snickered at my dirt-trapped-under-a-manicured-nail status. I filled the slot of the pre-show spectacle. I ignored them by moving to another bench, where I pretended to study the program. When that didn't work, I escaped to the bathroom. Two followed me in and spoke loudly about my hideous clothing while I hid in a stall.

My mother had loaned me the frock and helped me prepare. I'd trusted her uncharacteristic kindness when I should have known she had set me up to be mocked. Everything my mother touched turned to lead. I waited in the washroom until closer to curtain time to make my way to my seat.

By the time my friend Nicole showed up, I was an inconsolable wreck. She walked me to the lobby where my father happened to be waiting. He had decided it wasn't worth his time to go home. Nicole hugged me goodbye and said she'd call me the next day. I barely heard her promise.

I paused, and Dr. Salima jotted down a note.

"The worst part is how I can still hear them talking about me."

"Of course. That's what you've learned from your mother, but that's her problem, not yours. Does what I'm saying make sense?"

I frowned. "Not really."

"Your mother has schizophrenia, and if she came here, I wouldn't be able to help her. You don't have schizophrenia, but you learned from your mother how to behave, how to respond when you felt threatened. This is not particular to you, we all learn from our families. You, I can help."

I focused on the aloe vera plant on her desk. Finally, I broke the silence. "Will this take long?"

"The appointments are an hour."

"I mean, how long will I need to come for?"

"That's really up to you. To both of us."

I leaned back in the plush chair, relieved. Stories of people going to psychiatrists for years worried me; I hoped six months of weekly meetings could prevent me from losing my mind.

For the next two years, every Friday after school I took the bus north, the opposite direction from home, to meet with Dr. Salima. Each week I sat in the comfortable chair opposite her imposing wooden desk and tried to make sense of the absurd or the plain awful.

She listened attentively, and advised on how to cope with my mother's wrath.

In the time since the diagnosis, months that turned into years, my mother had grown more paranoid, more disturbed, more violent, harder to handle. I responded by retaliating with mindless force: when she wouldn't drink her medication one night, I threw it in her face, the orange juice mixture dripping onto her nightgown and bed sheets as she shrieked at me. She chased me down the hall and around the dining table where my father was reading the Italian paper.

He moaned, "O Dio, when will we have peace in this house? Lucy, take your medicine."

By then, I'd lost faith that my father would put an end to my mother's savagery even though he kept insisting I didn't need to worry, that he'd figure out a solution to the situation.

She lunged across him to reach for me and crumpled his newspaper.

In a fit of frustration, he stood. "I'm going for an espresso. Who can live like this?"

I said nothing. My mother waited for him to leave and cornered me in the living room. I turned and struck the side of her head with my fist.

She kicked at my knee.

I punched her ear again.

She grabbed my forearm and bit hard.

I fought back, scratching across her neck to force her jaw open.

Days when I couldn't muster the stamina needed to defend myself, I beat a hasty retreat, calling friends for help from the phone in my bedroom. When I was thirteen, my friend Athena had rushed over on her bicycle and ushered me out of the house; now at seventeen, we went to different high schools and had fallen out. She'd befriended a girl who detested me, and in the period that followed, I recognized Athena's domineering presence and petulant temper as a kinder-hearted version of my mom.

I told Dr. Salima about a recent fight. I'd barely made it to my room and had managed to shove a dresser against the door as my mother tried to crash through. Her right arm stuck in the doorway. The lock my father installed as a protective measure had broken months before during a different argument when my mother kicked the door open, breaking the wooden frame and metal latch. Pinned between the wall and the doorway, she screamed a slew of obscenities.

"Let me in," she shouted, hollering about what she would do with me when she got through the door. Three routine threats spun through her limited repertoire: she'd kill me, maim me and make me sorry I was ever born.

"I'm sorry you're my mother—get away from me!" I braced my shoulder against the side of the dresser and pressed my strength forward. "Go away!"

My mother's arm slammed repeatedly between the door and the frame. I could see the limb whiten as it was squeezed, as I pushed back.

She yowled. A pitch I imagined a wolf caught in a leg hold

trap would make. As the cause of her pain, I relented.

As soon as she felt my resolve weaken, she owned the brawl. She bulldozed the obstructed door and clambered over the dresser.

"You want to fight me, ingrate? Disagree with me? Test me? I'll teach you a lesson you'll never forget."

She screamed her favourite insults. "You weren't born, you came into the world as shit! You understand? I shit you out of me. You're nothing but a piece of shit. You think you can beat me? Garbage whore. You want a fight, I'll give you a fight, you gypsy slut." She landed blow after blow.

I curled on the floor like an armadillo, waiting for her to tire. I kept my head covered and kicked out when I could. One punt to her side knocked her off-balance. She fell next to me. Lashing out like a feral cat, she latched on to the forearm I'd flung across my face for protection with her mouth, sunk her teeth into the soft fleshy part and growled.

"Ma va fanculo — Let go, you raving fucking lunatic — "

"I'll teach you a lesson you'll never forget!"

"Go ahead psychopath — " I shrilled. "I'll dance on your grave when you're gone."

This stopped her cold. Her eyes narrowed. She threw back her head and chortled.

"What the hell is the matter with you?"

Repeatedly, she responded with belly laughs when she pushed me beyond my breaking point — that ledge I clung to until I tumbled into a chasm of sorrow and returned to lash out with rampant animosity. She goaded me until she got what she wanted: a nasty reaction. Each scuffle replenished her insatiable desire for another, and every time I stooped to her level of cruelty, she rejoiced. Engaged in one altercation after another,

I felt stuck in an eternal staring contest with my mother. I always blinked. She always won.

She stood up and pulled the dresser back into position and then left the room, still laughing, as if we'd watched a hilarious comedy routine.

I panted as I dialled my father's number at work. I never called him there, but I had the number in my nightstand drawer. The receptionist at the factory could barely understand me through my tears. She'd have to make an announcement over the PA system, since my father worked on the main floor. From her tone, I understood that this was a considerable inconvenience, and against protocol. Heavy machinery in the factory generated a high volume of white noise, the type found on construction sites. She hinted that it was dangerous. No one received calls on the job.

I pleaded, "It's an emergency."

My father answered the phone in an anxious tone, "Lucy? What's happened?"

"Papa—"

"Oh, thank God," relief flooded through my dad's voice.

I told him I couldn't take it anymore. Huddled on the floor with my arms wrapped around my legs, I stammered out the details.

"Don't provoke her."

"What did you say?"

"Don't upset her. When I come home, it will be another world war again. Every night it's a fight. I want a peaceful life. I'm at work. I can't do anything from here."

I couldn't believe what I was hearing. My father, a traitor siding with the enemy.

"You have to stay calm. You know how she is."

"Meh tu si pazz. You're crazy. Thanks for nothing, Dad."

"Nothing? I sacrifice my life and work so you can have a future, and this is what I get? You say thanks, this effort is nothing? I give you nothing? You don't know what it means to have nothing."

I held the receiver away from my ear and stared at it. My father's voice sounded frayed.

"Never mind." I slammed the phone down. I crawled under the covers and faced the wall until the outside dark took over the room.

Hours later, the garage door creaked open and shut. I said nothing when he came into my room to ask if I was mad at him. I couldn't acknowledge his presence. He stormed off sputtering that he worked hard and deserved peace and quiet. I skipped dinner, ignored both my parents' requests to come downstairs to eat. Worn out, I fell asleep in my jeans.

Retelling the story to Dr. Salima, my cheeks warmed with mortification. Even in her cool office, a sweat broke out around my hairline.

Dr. Salima listened and took notes. She placed her clipboard on to her desk and leaned forward to explain: one third of people who developed schizophrenia would improve, one third worsened, one third stayed the same.

I couldn't calculate. "So, my mother? Which one will she be?"

Dr. Salima brushed her hand across her lap, clearing invisible crumbs from her skirt. "From what we've talked about, from what you've told me, she'll get worse."

I stared at her, shaking my head. I couldn't imagine worse.

There were events I kept from Dr. S—the visit to the palm reader who predicted I would marry young, have three kids and travel the world. The weekly habit I'd developed of pulling out the Rider-Waite Tarot deck and attempting to forecast my fate. I found the cards at a bookstore in the flashy suburban Etobicoke mall and performed multiple Celtic Cross readings for myself—a complex ten card spread that detailed past strife, present woes and the possible future.

She removed her glasses, and cleaned them with a small cloth. A suggestion: leave home, pick a university in another province, settle down and get rooted in a place far, far away from both my parents.

"I can't. I don't think I can leave my dad."

"I think you can. I think you'll have to."

WHEEL of FORTUNE.

Wheel of Fortune
(X)

She spins the karmic roulette
and decides to leave.

Twice in my life, I've been cast as a citizen of Thebes under the rule of Oedipus. The first occasion was a high-school production I badgered my parents to attend. I spent the autumn of grade twelve chattering about playwriting and playacting, never catching on to their confusion. I ramped up my excitement when a drama teacher selected my script for production and entry to the Sears Ontario Drama Festival. I breezed around the house with newfound confidence. The show I would act in and the show I'd written were seventeen days apart. My lucky number: everything would work out fine—brilliant.

As a member of the chorus, I dressed in a hooded cloak with my face painted white and black to resemble a skeleton. I crawled across the auditorium stage in this harbinger of doom costume with eleven other teenage girls as the curtains parted.

In mournful unison, we yelled out "Plague!" and "Pestilence!" We moaned and growled. Enter Oedipus our king, the man who solved the Sphinx's riddle and saved Thebes from destruction. In this case, an eighteen-year-old teenager who called us children. I convulsed in torment as best I could, another theatre kid without any dance training rolling around for the sake of art.

A fog machine pumped out misty smoke. The smog of our ill-fated city flowed out into the audience.

My immigrant parents sat at the end of a row near the front of the crowd, bewildered.

Driving home afterwards they were unusually quiet. Stopped at a red light, my father looked over his shoulder to ask, aghast, "That's the play you was write?"

"I no like," said my mom.

"You guys think I wrote a story about a man who killed his father and married his mother?"

"I really no like," she repeated. "Ma perchè l'ha fatte?"

"Di che? Why did we put on a Greek tragedy or why did Oedipus commit murder?"

She sighed. "I really no was like nothing. Ne se capive niede." Nothing made sense.

My dad let out a relieved laugh. "Thank God. I was asking myself where from you take this idea."

The following month, my parents chose not to attend the play I had written. *The Last Moon* was an exploration of abuse, alienation and loneliness between two teen girls in a psych ward for adolescents that would go on to win a provincial drama festival award.

"Probably," said my mother, "we're not going to like it or understand what you wrote. Better if we stay home."

My father's silence on the subject meant that for the first time ever, they were in agreement.

By my last year of high school, I knew Dr. Salima was right. I applied to universities in Ontario and set my hopes on the one in Victoria, British Columbia. Putting 3,000 miles and a body of water between us calmed me. In *The House with a Clock in Its Walls*, a beloved book I renewed from the library many times as a girl, the main characters eluded a fiendish spirit in a car chase when their vehicle drove across a bridge. Evil couldn't cross running water. Sussing out the geography in an atlas, I hoped the Strait of Georgia would suffice.

I promised dad I would be gone for a year to engineer my escape. I'd had a taste of freedom before: a sleepover here and there; a grade seven school trip to Hockley Valley; two week-long high-school trips to Greece and France; six weeks of French immersion in Chicoutimi, Quebec (which is not enough to get you into the French Foreign Legion). Twelve months in Lotus Land—utter bliss.

I heard that it hardly snowed there. A friend's sister referred to the picturesque city as the place for the "newlywed and nearly dead." No matter. I pictured palm trees and sandy beaches; the narrow image I conjured of islands was a cartoon. I would hit the books while sipping a drink from a coconut or downing a piña colada; I deluded myself with visions of student life tantamount to spring break. I'd study the classics stretched out on a towel, reading Dante after slathering on suntan lotion.

I had a habit of tuning out, daydreaming and not paying attention when situations got sticky. But then the reckoning came, a moment when I woke up to reality with the illusion crushed.

In this case, the sandcastle I mentally built could easily be swept out with the tide. Still, I reasoned, anything was better than the life I lived with my parents.

When the acceptance letter arrived, I celebrated by going out to lunch at Swiss Chalet with my friend Nicole.

I counted the days to my departure like a castaway carving lines into a single coconut tree, and stuffed a large suitcase with summer clothes and jeans.

My mother declined my request for one set of bedsheets from the four in my mothball-scented dowry. I argued that it was stupid to spend money on new linens: she countered that I could stay in Toronto and get married. She'd been browbeating the subject of matrimony since I'd turned sixteen.

I said, "Nice try, but not a chance."

She followed me out of the spare bedroom as I twirled down the hallway and danced my best version of the Charleston in the kitchen. I pulled her into a polka like the ones she'd loved to watch on *The Lawrence Welk Show*. We spun around until she was dizzy with laughter and pushed me away.

"But why did you have to pick a place so far away?"

"You know why. We never get along for very long. No matter what I do. No matter how hard I try to make you happy."

"All families fight."

"Not like us." I went back to my room without saying another word.

One of my mother's most maddening qualities was an ability to wipe her memory slate clean of blame for her atrocious behaviour. Her demeanour lurched from furious to unruffled in seconds: a process unnerving to witness, and one that kept me in a state of perpetual confusion. How did the rage dissipate?

Where did the malice get buried? How could I avoid tripping onto the minefield next time? My mother delighted in expressing rage. Finally it occurred to me that her rancour-filled tantrums released all the toxins she carried within.

No action I could take in the present would mend my mother or soothe her psychosis. We would never have a made-for-tv-movie moment of recognition and repair the harm that harnessed us to each other—a clichéd event I'd been waiting for my entire life. The no-win situation is a maelstrom. An anathema to stories of survival, resilience and overcoming adversity. The world wants the hero's journey, not a leper's struggle.

In early August, all three of us went to Pearson International, where we had over two hours to skulk around until check-in time. In keeping with my father's habit, we had arrived at the airport hours ahead of the recommended time—earliness a tendency I learned from him, a man who rose and went to work at 6 AM for forty-six years without ever once owning an alarm clock.

Throughout high school, my English teachers had encouraged me to write, and I'd won an award for my efforts, so a schoolmate (Greg, aka his majesty, Oedipus Rex) and I were flying to the land down under to attend a conference for young playwrights in Sydney, Australia. My father groused about the expensive trip and then paid for the excursion. He fretted that my burgeoning creative adventures would lead me astray while I stargazed a life spent surrounded by authors, books, and countless cups of tea. After Oz, I would go to Victoria and start school.

My mother pulled out a handkerchief and dabbed her eyes. She blew her nose as if it were a trumpet. Her face puckered like she'd bitten into a lime wedge, the fruit I pictured garnishing my first beverage after I took up residence in a happy place for good. Her eyes scrunched up, and she wailed: a deafening noise.

"Oh Dio Sante, Dio Sante!" She launched into the spiel she'd maintained since my application to university out West. "But why? Why?" The last word she elongated, blaring like a wartime air-raid siren.

My father said, "Lucia, please. Ma ne vede che stai irritare a tutti? A tua figlia?"

Of course, she could see she was upsetting me. I assumed that was the point.

To the average Giuseppe, all the travelers standing around waiting for their own take-off, I must have seemed glacial and stone-hearted. A Shakespearian villain demanding the pound of flesh closest to my mother's heart.

Her exhibition particularly galled me after the eons I'd spent as a human punching bag. Aside from a few occurrences of tenderness and instances of tempting me onto her team by acting like we were co-conspirators cut from the same cloth, she went for the jugular. When she trashed me verbally, attacked me physically, I felt like a walking waste bin, a receptacle for discarded eggshells and coffee grounds.

Now she expected sympathy? An ostrich feather could have toppled me.

My friend Olivia showed up to see me off. Her humour and friendship had been a balm through the last hellish year of high school. She had been talking to me on the phone in April when my mother stormed into my bedroom. She'd been listening in on the extension downstairs, and I told her to get off the phone. We stopped talking until we heard the click. Less than a minute later, I was fending my rabid mother off as she tried to strangle me.

Olivia gave me a quizzical look and jerked her chin over to my mom.

The grief show had gained pyrotechnic power, a fireworks festival in human form: "Oh my daughter, my daughter. My only daughter." She cried out in English. "Why she have to leave home without her Mamma? Why she leave home? Why she leave me? O Dio santé, Dio santé. Give me strength. I no can take no more. I no know what I do."

My jaw ached from clenching my mouth shut. A faint twitching on the side of my eye, one that had pestered me for months, renewed with vigour.

An airport security guard came to check on the commotion: I saw him walking toward us and felt my stomach contort.

"Papa," I stared at my father, furious with him afresh. Appealing to my mother was useless. "Forze e meglio se te ne vade." I thought it best they left.

"E mo —" he shrugged. He didn't want to leave.

I stared at the ground, looked around to the end of the terminal. I shook my head at him, livid. My mother's tears were fake. Lacrime di coccodrillo. And he, the lone persistent witness of my torment, was willing to let me endure this last indignity. He too wanted to hang on, to cleave; I wanted to jump on the plane and tell the pilot "Let's go. I mean gun it, buddy. Get me the hell outta Dodge as fast as you can."

I refused to acknowledge my parents, and chitchatted with Olivia. The classmate accompanying me to Oz showed up. He gaped at my mom. I held my passport, rubbing my thumb over the cover. A worry stone. My ticket to run away from the circus.

I couldn't fathom why my mother would behave so outlandishly like a loving parent. I fumed and staved off her one-woman opera of wretchedness, along with multiple attempts to yank me into a hug. She kept kissing my cheeks as if I were reporting for combat duty and about to meet certain death.

When her words failed to have an effect, she clutched her head and keened: a living, breathing version of Edvard Munch's painting *The Scream* stood before me.

"Come on, Ma, don't be like that."

I wanted to tell the security officer and all the others who slowed down and kept turning to look at the train wreck, "My mother has suffered from an aggressive psychosis since before I was born. She's constantly harassed by auditory hallucination. She's volatile. Four months ago, she tried again to kill me. This miss-me routine is new. Untested. Not an audience pleaser. I'm begging you to ignore us."

My classmate and I got in line for the departure gate. The airport crowd edged closer to my escape doorway.

Greg's family, having said their goodbyes, stood by quietly as we progressed slowly up the line moving through the security gate.

Everyone looked sad except for me: I seethed with frustration and impatience. My mother's wailing acted as the tuning fork for everyone's distress except mine.

Greg turned to me. "I had no idea you could be so cold."

I glared at him. "Enjoy the show."

The plane had been in the air for an hour when I thought: she'd hoped to mortify me into staying.

Justice
(XI)

*She encounters an adjudicator
who weighs in on the past.*

Initially, my father did not want me to attend school far
away. He relented saying, "My cousin Rocco is there. He
promised to look after you."

I'd never heard of the man before selecting Victoria as a
sanctuary. We had additional family in Canada? The wedge
my mother had driven into my connections in Toronto were too
damaged to salvage. The youngest and sole female, and having
gone through a short-lived stage as a Goth at sixteen, some of
my older male cousins found me spoiled or plain weird. I was a
mess, and my cousins had their own hyphenated world to wres-
tle: Italo-Canuck. The first generation born or raised away from
the ancestral land inhabits a borderland, dangling between two
countries, two cultures. Effectively exiled from one and tentatively embraced into the other.

My dad's older cousin had lived on Vancouver Island since

immigrating to Canada in the 1950s, almost a full decade before my father.

The news distressed me. If I'd spun a globe and my finger landed on Moscow, my father might have replied, "No problem, we have family there too." Imagining a planet populated with thousands of relatives left me weary to the bone.

How would I escape? Who planned a getaway to find out close relations resided in the oasis?

Rocco's father and my dad's father, Nonno Gennaro, had been brothers.

Their mothers had been sisters.

A rustic romance. The next layer: they were also first cousins.

Don't judge. Royalty did it all the time. I'm sorry if this is news, but somewhere in everyone's ancestry is a set of first cousins who married. The difference with my grandparents (and Rocco's parents) was that they had fallen in love, had chosen a love match at a time when most Italian unions were arranged. Nonno Gennaro broke a promise made by his father to a wealthy landowner and chose to marry Femia: his decision forced my great-grandfather to sell off farmland in order to return the dowry.

"We're really close, then. He's your cousin two times, two ways."

"He's my favourite. When he soldiered in the army, he send me postcards from everywhere he was go."

A power shortage caused a blackout at Vancouver Airport. Stranded in a pitch-dark public washroom, I couldn't even see my hands as I groped along the wall with several other women to walk out. In the main area outside the women's washroom, emergency backup lights from a generator dimly lit the area.

An airport announcement mentioned an outage problem. At the baggage carousel, I learned that my suitcase had not made the journey.

I filled out a claim, found my way to the bus to the ferry, and didn't think of my address book until I was on the boat crossing the strait. Rocco's phone number and address were inside the notebook perched on the sink. I had pulled it out of my backpack and set it down seconds before the lights went out. On the flight from Sydney to Los Angeles and then LA to Vancouver, I tried to get some shut-eye and couldn't, so I was fighting exhaustion.

In my jean jacket pocket, I found a slip of paper with the phone number of a friend's sister in Victoria. I called collect from the ferry. The sister was at work, and I could hear a party in full swing at the house. I cried. Wiped out, I explained to her roommate who I was, how the airline had lost my luggage, and that I'd lost the address in Victoria of my relative. Rebecca showed up at the bus depot with another reveller, holding up a sign with my name. Back at the house, people kept offering me pizza and going on at length about the main ingredient, mushrooms. Everyone, it seemed, was a pizza-with-mushrooms fanatic. They also offered homemade brownies. I declined it all, too tired to eat. I sat down on the couch and conked out while the partiers carried on around me.

In the morning, I woke up groggy and unsure of my surroundings. I lay stretched out on the couch. Someone had thrown a blanket over me and put a pillow under my head, gestures I hadn't noticed at all. Normally a light sleeper, I checked my wristwatch and realized I'd been out for almost twelve hours. I sat up with a start, and found a phone in the kitchen to call my parents collect.

My mother answered yelling, "Where you are?"

My father got on the downstairs extension. He said, "I no sleep, worry all night something happen — "

I apologized for not calling.

"You better be call Rocco. He was think to call the police."

"Please, can you stop now? I'm okay, I'm safe."

My father repeated Rocco's number to me and insisted I call him immediately.

Rocco's loud voice boomed even when I held the receiver away from my ear. "Where you been? Why don't you phone me when you got in last night? You know what you was put your father through? And me? We didn't know where you was or what's happen."

"Stop yelling at me. I already talked to my dad."

"I thank God I never had a daughter!"

"I thank God too. You probably would have ruined her life."

Silence as he takes in what I've said. He ignored the insult and arranged to pick me up the following week for dinner. His wife was in the hospital recuperating from major surgery; her left leg had been amputated below the knee a week before I arrived.

I dressed to meet them as if I were attending Easter Mass, trying to undo the terrible first impression of a depraved daughter who didn't care about familial duty or respect for her elders. I waited outside my apartment building on Rockland Ave. Rocco drove by in a bright blue pickup. He pointed at me as he passed, wagging his finger at me. I recognized his angular Italian profile, his gesture, as an echo of family. By then, I'd turned him into a mythical long-lost relation, one I couldn't believe existed. Like happening upon a misplaced treasured item, I gasped. I covered my mouth and then, feeling self-conscious, offered a timid wave. He turned and pulled into the driveway next to me.

"I was think I see a ghost. You look like your grandmother, the exact same face. When I see you, I see my aunt."

"That's what everyone tells me."

Rocco's wife, Colleen, was waiting for us at the hospital. Rocco helped steady her on crutches and took us to Ming's Restaurant on Quadra Street.

Rocco struck me as remarkably familiar and incredibly different. His accent was thick, but his English and grammar skills were infinitely better than my parents. I chalked up his fluency to immersion in an Anglo community and a second marriage to an Irish woman. My parents never went out for dinner. We'd been served seven-course meals at weddings, had attended communion and confirmation parties, but dinner in a sit-down restaurant was a foreign experience.

We tried it once, when I was eight. My father had been invited to dine at an upscale steak house in exchange for his masterful presentation on the art of butchery. I ordered French onion soup because I thought it would help me understand the language. My mother was beautiful in a pale blue sleeveless dress with a skirt that flared out and swished when she walked. She ignored the waiter and rebuked every attempt my father made at ordering for her. She pressed her lips together, shook her head and refused to speak for the rest of the evening. She stared at the other guests until they squirmed. My father urged me to stop slurping my soup, and we left quickly. My dad tipped generously for the free meal. On our way out, he apologized to the server.

Rocco piled his plate high with mixed vegetables, fried rice and pieces of lemon chicken. "Your mom and dad worry about you."

"Well my dad does." I gave a truncated version of my autobiography: the torment my father tolerated.

Rocco paused mid-chew and looked me over. He took in my seersucker dress, studied my made-up face. I stared back, determined not to blink. He broke away first, shaking his head, and I notched a small victory.

"I no believe. Your grandfather Joe helped me come to Canada." He proceeded to lecture me on the merits of my mother's relatives. Nonno Baron, Joe, was a hard worker, a man who did well by his wards, a man who was great with the farming and finance business, saving everything he earned, and becoming an astute moneylender to the economic refugees fleeing Molise. "That's how he earned 'The Baron' as a nickname."

"That doesn't mean he's a good father." My face turned cherry-red as I grew forceful with my opinion. "That doesn't mean Sapooch and Barone are decent people. They're crude, ignorant peasants."

Rocco's mouth dropped open. My disrespect offended him deeply. "What do you know about raising a family? What do you know about keeping your kids alive during a war or in the aftermath? When the soil's been torched and the livestock slaughtered?"

"Absolutely nothing. But I'm not lying."

"It's good you came to study writing with this imagination."

"Ask your cousin. He'll tell you the same."

Colleen continued eating, glancing sideways at Rocco and then across the table at me. An ex-nun, perhaps she too thought I deserved a fire and brimstone afterlife.

"I don't know nothing about what you say." Rocco chewed and swallowed. He shook his head again. "Sorry, but I can't believe you."

)

The rest of dinner passed with small talk, questions about my theatre and literature courses. I was polite and remote, already deciding I would have nothing to do with this newly met branch of the family tree. I had distanced myself from my mother's family in Montreal and Italy. I wasn't close to my cousins in Toronto. Cutting myself off was too easy; no one seemed to care about the canyon-sized gulf of confusion and misunderstanding between us. Bridges weren't burned by my mother's rampages, they were carpet-combed. Her diagnosis effected no change. She refused medication. In her fury, she'd racked up restraining orders, assault charges and shoplifting offenses.

Simply being in British Columbia meant she had failed in her efforts to stall my education and ensnare me in a miserable future.

For Rocco, I was a mystery he couldn't solve. As far as he knew, the offspring of his good-natured cousin was a pathological liar. A female Pinocchio whose fibs were as plain and large and similar as the nose on her face was to his.

I remained silent during the lift back to my apartment. I wondered if I had no real family besides my father; beyond blood ties, familiar faces, builds or mannerisms, everyone was a stranger.

I stood at the steps of my building and waved goodbye until Rocco's truck disappeared around the corner. I went upstairs and lay on my futon mattress, falling asleep without getting undressed.

He called two days later to invite me to dinner. "You have to meet the whole family."

I stalled, but couldn't think of any reason to give; other than my roommate, I hadn't met anyone through my classes. I hadn't even realized how shy I was until this move to another province.

"Listen, I talk with your dad." Rocco cleared his throat. "I phoned him to say 'I think there's something wrong with your daughter.' Because what you was told me... "

I picked at my fingernails with my thumb as he spoke. My lips pursed.

"I told him what you was say. Your father said is true—tells me worse things. So listen, I'm sorry I no was believe you before."

I broke down.

Rocco yelled, "Don't cry! You're here now! That life is finish so what you cry for now? There nothing to cry for here, okay? You come for dinner. I'm cook spaghetti."

I wiped my cheeks with the back of my arm. Getting the sobbing under control caused me to hiccup. "You can cook?"

"Yes, I can cook. What's the matter with you?"

Rocco, I would observe, had adapted to the modern world more than my father. Nine years older, he acted as an affable big brother to my dad. I started calling him uncle. Loud, gregarious and hilarious, he took on the role of my father-away-from-home with gusto. He called to remind me to call him, called to invite me to dinner, called because he wanted to know "What's gone on?"

My first three months in Victoria, I ran up a $900 phone bill calling high-school friends who'd scattered to different cities and provinces. It rained twenty out of thirty days that November; the damp lingered in my towels, my shoes and my spirit. Early December, I called home crying. I was failing poetry and miserably lonely. I'd stopped attending creative writing classes, the one subject that could still make my pulse flicker with excitement. I called at three in the morning Toronto time; I woke my parents. Both scrambled to comfort me over the phone. Both said, "Come home."

I kept them on the phone until I felt exhausted enough to fall asleep.

Later the same morning, at 8 AM, Rocco called and woke me. "You crazy or what? You know how much your parents worry? Next time you feel bad, you call me. Don't matter what time, three, four in morning, you understand me? You phone me, and I come and get you. Understand?"

I let out a sob. Then another and another. "Yeah, I understand."

"Okay, don't cry. If you're going to cry, I'm no going to come. I'll leave you there, crying by yourself. Tonight you come for dinner. Five-thirty. Don't be late."

The Hanged Man (XII)

She pauses to reflect, regroup, and reveal.

The truth: escaping the murky past is mystifying. Anxiety followed me everywhere, shadowing every move, there at the edges of every planned next step. Running away from trouble, or running toward trouble—the point, I guessed, was that trouble would find me. I developed habits and patterns of thinking, sometime ruts of behaviour to cope. And it was impossible to escape Italian parents who called weekly to complain and carp long-distance. The dismay lived inside me: my nervous stomach. The panic-spiraling thought process that looped through my days and nights. The way I flinched at the loud voices of passersby. I fidgeted with my clothes, pulling my sleeves over my hands, my T-shirt over my lips. Only later did I realize my body language spoke of cloaking and remaining hidden. I did my best to hide from the past, but it found me again and again, in distressing dreams, in messy relationships.

When I sat down to write, every story contained conflict with a difficult mother.

Two years into my Victoria life, my friend and roommate, Frances, recommended the university's free counselling services after I ruined her good mood with another night of lamenting.

Every Sunday morning conversation with my parents drained me. My father grumbled about my mother nonstop. She called and criticized, called and ranted, called and left dreadful messages on the answering machine. The grey days and incessant rain in Victoria took on a Dickensian quality in winter; the sensation spread to summer. I never wanted to go out. I didn't even want to get out of bed. I needed a job, and there were none.

Rocco called with an invitation to dinner and berated my lack of initiative. "Go downtown to the Employment Centre. If no one has work, grab a broom and start sweeping the floor right there. They'll see you're serious about finding work. You better not stay inside. It's no good living like this. You need to keep busy."

It didn't help that the local paper published a cover story stating there were hundreds of positions and not enough students to fill them.

My uncle read the article. "What's the matter with you?"

"I don't know. I don't have any energy. All my muscles ache all the time, even when I get up in the morning."

"Eufemia, I'm tell you something important, and you better listen. There is nothing wrong with you. You need a job, okay? That's all."

Though suspicious, I made an appointment with the counselling office. Nothing came free, everything had a price. A woman named Kate, with long straight hair and a striking resemblance to Juice Newton welcomed me. She was a doctoral student, working on her practicum. I followed her into a small room where she explained the format: three complimentary sessions, forty-five minutes each, with a possibility they would refer me to someone if after that amount of guidance I still felt in need of assistance. I almost laughed in her face. I'd spent nearly four years with Dr. Salima, right up until the last year of high school when she weaned me off by double-booking newer clients in my appointment time. She wanted me to practice independence and confidence. Losing her sympathetic ear had been a blow.

In point form, I gave Kate my top three concerns from the greatest hits list. In response to her quizzical stare, I rushed through an explanation: my mother's propensity to attack people was probably the result of being raised in an abusive home back in Italy.

"I don't subscribe to the theory that violence begets violence. Simply because one is raised in that environment doesn't mean they have to perpetuate the awful behaviour. That would mean violence is a type of unbroken circle."

I frowned, wrinkling my forehead. "What if they had no other examples? No good role models?"

"Everyone has a choice."

"My mother grew up in the aftermath of the Second World War. In a country that was devastated by a dictator. My parents were shoved together like Ken and Barbie dolls. They didn't have the luxury of choosing to go to school." I couldn't veil the annoyance in my voice and sounded pompous as I promoted History 201: The Italian Campaign.

Kate clasped her hands and let them fall onto her lap. She leaned back before she spoke again, her words clipped for emphasis. "Everyone always has a choice."

I told myself this was typical of the hogwash I could expect from the clueless. I should have known. People mistook my traditional, old-fashioned name for a moniker they thought counterculture flower children folks had bestowed on me. Or they assumed "Italian" meant marble statues, operas, carnival and high culture. My parents' Italy was a place of small-town suspicion and historic misfortune.

My voice shook. "No they don't. Marriages get arranged. Lives get destroyed. What choices can those people make?"

She shrugged. She couldn't help me if I wasn't willing to listen to her rationale.

In desperation, I kept the next two appointments where Kate continued to advocate agency. I left despondent. I had dropped creative writing but stayed in school, unable to focus on any of my courses. I showed up sporadically for Theatre History, Technology in Education and Latin class. My central nervous system felt plugged into the old Emergency Broadcast System that played on television during my childhood. I kept waiting for instructions—where to go and what to do: If life was a test, I was failing.

The brief dip into psychological aid didn't diminish any of my anxiety. In every sense, it expanded the stress: My right eye twitched during each appointment. I wondered what that meant in the old-world wisdom my parents tried to impart.

Four months later, after another nudge from Frances, I got a therapist. Doug booked me into several biweekly sessions and suggested I also join group therapy: "Where the real work begins."

In one group meeting, Doug allowed a graduate student to come in and ask questions. She was studying aspects of shared memory, specifically how two family members could experience the same event and yet remember it differently. I sat on the couch, stone-hearted, irritated with the changed agenda. I disliked this grad-gal. My age, she had her life together, working on a thesis, building a career. I was back in therapy, feeling stuck again. I signed up for group to "come to terms with" my issues, afraid life would never work out. Nothing would change. I would be weeping about the same old scars, the same unhealed wounds forever. One day my parents would die: One day I would be dead. I figured then, definitely, things would have to change. Death, according to an instructor, was an adjustment in the individual's cosmic address. Did I have to wait that long for the gloom to subside?

The grad student handed out questionnaires. "Don't record any memory where your head sustained an injury. If you fell and hit your head, or if you were struck by a ball or—"

"Or what?" I prodded. She didn't need to complete the sentence. This was a room full of people who understood the myriad possibilities of being struck. I checked the paper and decided it was a no-brainer. I couldn't participate. No answers unless I could write "Shove it" as an answer to each question.

Doug looked over and saw me sitting with my arms folded across my chest, my lips pressed in a line of grim determination.

He cocked his head in query.

I looked away. Hadn't he paid attention when I spoke? All my memories contained potential head slaps, cuffs and jabs. My face flushed pink. What was the point of this young woman's research? Substantiating False Memory Syndrome? Did this mean most of my memories wouldn't be believed? That I would be viewed as untrustworthy? My thoughts clouded with confusion and frustration. I wasn't interested in being a lab rat, poked and tested to see if I could find my way out of someone's textbook labyrinth.

After the student had left, Doug asked the group, "How was that? Did you witness how you responded to change? What did you learn?"

"Nothing. If you must know. Absolutely nothing."

Heads turned to look at me.

I shook my head. "Seriously, what was the point?"

Doug examined his fingernails. "So you should do what makes you comfortable, is that it? Is that why you're here?"

"I don't know why I'm here. I know I don't like having my time wasted."

I lasted until I couldn't take the group-therapy-speak anymore. Frequently, palpable friction occurred when members triggered each other, and I recognized the innately human habit of comparison. Occasionally someone would note the toxic impact my mother had and would ask why I didn't cut off contact. Fatigue weighed me down every time I had to translate the elements of my personal universe: daughter plus duty, the first generation, disconnection from both sides of the family, my lifelong yearning to fit in and longing to belong. At twenty-two, one of the youngest members of the group, I was pouring over the past like a senior who'd messed up every opportunity given. I couldn't shake off the sense of dread that accompanied me everywhere.

Doug would ask over and over, "Whose script is it?"

And my reply: "Mine," or "My dad's," or "My mother's" or "I don't have a clue, tell me." There were no answers in Doug's office, merely questions. And I could come up with those on my own, gratis, without handing over the money my father deposited in my bank account.

Years later, when I finally returned to school to complete my studies and concentrate on drafts of my own thesis, a writing mentor asked, "Whose story is it?"

I didn't hesitate: "Mine. My folks have starring roles."

Death

(XIII)

She wonders whether
chaos can be avoided.

The first time I saw a dead body, a girl of eight lay in a coffin, clad in her First Communion gown. Ringlets framed her heart-shaped face, and her cheeks were dusted a pale rose blush. She had a headpiece with a veil tucked beneath her hair. Her folded hands clutched a prayer book and a rosary that wove through her fingers.

A year older than me, she had drowned at the Alderwood Pool. My mother dragged me to the viewing against my father's expressed command. He thought the exposure to a deceased child would frighten me and inspire nightmares. Mom held my wrist and nudged us in front of others waiting to pay their respects. We knelt at the pew placed before the casket. She pulled me forward, forcing me to touch the cool, lifeless hands. In the mourners' receiving line, Mom introduced me to the grieving young mother as her greatest blessing. The woman covered her eyes and wailed.

My father found out about our jaunt. Someone he knew had attended the viewing and mentioned my mother's appalling lack of decorum.

He boxed her ears when he got home from the espresso bar.

As a young girl, I repeatedly asked my father for the story of Rizzoli: Walking back from the fields after another harvest day, my eight-year-old father led the way back to their house on Via Rosello. His preteen sisters and Gennaro followed at a short distance. They strode single file, taking a route along a dirt path bordered by high grass. Rizzoli, their German shepherd, snarled and barked. The dog leapt in front of dad, knocking him to the ground. A snake hidden in the tall greenery struck, biting Rizzoli's hind leg. My aunts yelled. Sofia grabbed her brother's elbow and heaved him away from the viper. Gennaro swore and stomped on the snake. Rizzoli lay on his side, panting out last breaths. Nonno cried as their animal guardian died.

My father would relate the cliff-hanger in three short sentences, ending with, "The dog was finish."

Each retelling, I pleaded for details. I wanted to live surrounded by stories, even scary ones.

"Who can remember? Was long times ago."

In my mind, I stitched together a narrative of his undocumented past, but too many missing puzzle pieces baffled me. "If you died, I couldn't be born. You couldn't be here. I couldn't be here. Then we couldn't be talking—"

"You wouldn't be bothering me—"

"Papa, how did that girl drown? How come no one saw her? No one saved her."

He frowned. "Oh, Chickpea. I don't know. Let's take a walk

to the Sunday store. Maybe the owner has new *Richie Rich* for you reading."

I wondered about my dad's fate, twice saved by Germans. The other was human: a soldier retreating through southern Italy as the Allied forces advanced. The Battle of Monte Cassino waged for six months until the occupying troops pulled up stakes and withdrew. Whenever they could, the withdrawing forces deployed a scorched-earth strategy, destroying everything in their wake.

The soldier saved my father from another soldier, a comrade gone crazy. Mussolini was dead. The platoon was beating a frantic path north through hostile territory, the blood-rich soil of Samnium.

One early morning, on the way to the fields, my six-year-old father, fourteen-year-old Rocco, Femia, her sister and their mother, Lina, stumbled across the platoon. Lina, my great-grandmother, pushed the boys behind her. Shielding them with her body, she stood defiant. She would not see her future, all her hopes destroyed.

One dishevelled young man advanced with his rifle drawn and aimed at the old woman and the children. He swung the barrel back and forth, unsure who to kill first. Another man stepped forward and signalled for the gun to be lowered. He negotiated through hand gestures, mimed eating to ask for food and pointed west to ask for directions.

The women handed over their bread.

The calm soldier directed the women and boys to stay put. He drew a finger across his own throat to demonstrate what would happen if they ran into my father and his family again.

Three years into my move west, I had a basic routine: I went to classes when I could muster the energy during the week and worked one day of the weekend at a gift shop. I spent the rest of the time sleeping or hanging out with friends.

Each Sunday my father would telephone, reciting a litany of my mother's transgressions. Then my mother would shout from the downstairs extension that she was sick of tolerating us, how we'd made her crazy. If they were particularly contentious, my parents would call separately, yelling at me about how impossible their life together was without my company. The phone in the living room would ring in the middle of the night or at five in the morning, waking my roommates, putting me in perpetual-apology mode. To my isolated mom, everything was urgent news she had to share, including the fact that she found underwear on sale at Bargain Harold's and wanted to mail the polyester briefs express post. I tried to stop answering the majority of their calls. I wanted to wean them off immediate access. Why couldn't they modernize and learn to leave a message on the newfangled technology: an answering machine.

The tape filled with baffling voicemails—both my parents spoke to the recorded voice as if I was listening in real time: "Eufemia, hello? Pick up the phone, it's Mamma. Hello? Why you no answer? You no there? Where you go?"

My plan backfired. My mother left rage-filled rants and spewed invectives. Sometimes she would still refer to me as my father's whore. I breathed a sigh of relief that none of my roommates understood Italian and purchased a beige push-button phone for my room so I could grab the receiver as soon as it rung.

Nothing good ever comes of the witching hour—between 3 and 4 in the morning—the time believed to be when most people are likely to die. It was half past the supernatural time slot when the phone on my nightstand jolted me out of a dream. Dazed with sleep, I murmured a hello-do-you-know-the-time-here?

My father was on the line. He sounded shattered. His normal baritone voice shook as he whispered feverishly. "I can't take no more. Come home. I'm finish. Come home and take care of your mother."

He'd been feeling off for months. His high blood pressure needed constant monitoring. Physically weakened and mentally feeble, he collapsed at work after a delusional hallucination that Christ was deeply disappointed in him. Convinced he'd offended God, my father was sent home from the factory and told no one what transpired: not his sisters, not his nephews, not me.

The strain in his voice should have snapped me awake. I stretched but didn't sit up, didn't shake myself out of slumber. "Papa? What's happening this time?"

"I can't take no more. I take already so much."

I repeat the words he spoke to me as a child. "Don't worry. It will be okay." I promised we'd talk and make a plan while I was home. Easter was a few days away, and I would be home for a visit after exams.

That was too late. It was too late. He'd waited too long, he said, and hung up.

I cradled the receiver and crashed out, falling back asleep shortly after turning onto my other side.

Noon the next day, I remembered the call, remembered it wasn't a strange dream. My heart raced as I recalled the disturbing timber of my father's voice, his anguished tone. I ran to my room and seized the receiver, dropping it on the floor.

My mother answered.

"Mamma, is everything okay?"

"Sure. Why?"

"Where's Papa? Let me talk to him."

"Oh, who knows where he went?" She said all my favourite dishes were being prepared for my upcoming trip.

"Tell Papa to call me as soon as he gets home."

He didn't.

I called again a couple of frantic hours later.

My father reluctantly got on the phone. His voice was flat, and he denied making the desperate call, cutting me off when I reminded him. "We'll talk when you're home."

Two weeks later, I boarded a red-eye flight to Toronto.

My cousin Vince came to the airport with my father to pick me up.

"What's going on? Is everything okay?" I couldn't even remember the last time I saw my cousin. It was always my parents greeting me at Pearson.

Vince kissed me on both cheeks. Chatty as a statue, he barely spoke during the car ride back to south Etobicoke. I caught his gaze in the rear view mirror, and he looked away.

"Can someone please tell me what's going on? Is everybody okay?"

"Sure everything is okay now you here." My dad turned around in the front passenger seat to squeeze my arm. He pinched my chin and noted I was plumper than I'd been at Christmas, when he and my mother had come out to the West Coast. In four months, he'd grown paler and less puffy. He'd lost a lot of weight. His hands trembled. He was fifty-one, and I thought: How did he get old so fast?

Vince dropped us off. "Maybe we should go see a movie while you're here. I'll call you."

My mouth fell open. I stammered a reply. "Sure. That

would be nice. Thank you."

My father hesitated before unlocking the door. "Try not to upset your Mamma."

There was a new aspect to his familiar worry-lined forehead. A factor in his weary expression I'd never seen before: he was afraid.

"Okay, Papa. Tell me. Cosa sta succedendo?"

"Nothing. No say nothing. Don't make her angry." His eyes held mine with undisguised panic. I thought back to the phone call and cursed myself for being lax. After years of basic boot camp on the home front, dealing with disastrous skirmishes, it turned out I couldn't recognize when a real crisis was about to hit. All the clues had been there: his tremulous voice, the dramatic weight gain and loss, the talk of preparing a will.

My mother had a lunch feast on the table. I protested; it wasn't even nine o'clock. She dished out a bowl of pastina and pushed provolone, crusty bread and olives in my direction. My father said little. He watched my mother's every move like a mouse sizing up a cat. She pestered him to eat as well, but he dismissed every offer. His hands shook as he drank a glass of water that he insisted on getting for himself. His chin quivered so much that splashes dripped onto his shirt.

I'd never seen anything like it: his jitteriness unnerved me. I knew my father craved peace, harmony and stillness, but now his body betrayed him. His movements jumpy and unsteady.

"I'm not flying overnight ever again." I hadn't caught any rest on the flight.

My mother cleared the table. "Your bed is made. Go sleep."

I woke an hour later to my father pacing anxiously up and down the hallway outside my bedroom.

"Come sit outside with me. We can talk there."

I splashed cold water onto my face and followed him to the picnic table in the backyard. Outside, a bright, sunny morning heralded the blossoms of a balmy spring, hotter than a West Coast April.

I sat down across from him. "Papa, really, what is happening? Why is everyone acting strange? I haven't seen Vince in six years."

"First, cross your feet like this." He demonstrated.

"Why?"

"If you don't, she might hear us."

"Who?"

He looked around the yard and then looked down at my slippered feet. I crossed my ankles.

"Mamma. She can still hear us when she's not here. Maybe even from ten, twenty, a hundred kilometres away. She can hear everything we say to each other. You have to keep your ankles crossed for what I'm about to tell you."

A sour taste overwhelmed my mouth. I hadn't brushed my teeth. I wrapped my arms around my waist. I tried to focus on my father's words while grappling with my inner voice: no. no. no. no. no. no. no. no. no. no.no.no.no.no.no.no. Not this. Not him too. He can't get sick. Please God, no.

"Over Easter, I was very sick. I was in St. Joe's Hospital." He explained: he'd collapsed again. This time he ended up in a psych ward.

"What do you mean again? When did you collapse the first time? Why didn't anyone call me? You were in the hospital, and nobody called me?" In shock, my pitch rose. All the muscles in my back and neck stiffened. This had to be rock-bottom. The lowest blow. My dad in jeopardy and no one in my family's inner circle of cousins, aunts and uncles filled me in? No one.

"Shhhh-shh-sh! Zitte! Don't get upset. Keep your voice down. Let me finish before your mother comes back."

Malocchio had sent him to the hospital. The evil eye, the curse that escorted our family through life.

"Papa, come on. You can't really believe that."

But he did and he always had, the belief so old, so embedded in the history of Southern Italy, passed down through every generation. In our family, the deadly malevolence caused by others was considered fact, not fiction. Spell-casters had spread virulent illnesses again, using sorcery identical to that which had slain his eldest sister as a toddler, his mother as a senior. He laid out his proof: Nonna Femia's planned trip to Canada for my First Communion had been curtailed when she took ill and died. He reminded me that I'd been afflicted too, as an infant. Of course I wouldn't remember, but my Aunt Sofia had removed the hex.

He described heaven-sent hallucinations as my mind strove to catch up. My gut churned with terror. I put my hand on my chest to calm myself, to still my quickening heart rate. Two mentally ill parents. I was doomed.

He blamed his mother-in-law, Sapooch, and his toxic marriage to her malicious daughter. They cursed him repeatedly, had tried to destroy him. He was full of self-recrimination for talking openly and often about his dissatisfaction with my mom. He said, "Mamma is extremely dangerous."

I stared at him, stunned. "You're just figuring this out now?"

My six-foot father—the malnourished kid who grew up to be a sturdy man—had an imposing physical presence, especially for people who didn't know how tenderhearted he was. And yet he trembled in terror.

Unsympathetic and unforgiving, I thought, no: my father could not lose his marbles. He had to pull himself together. I stood up to go back inside. "This is bullshit." I couldn't bear to look at him.

"Don't be like that," my father pleaded. "We've always gotten along. We always understood each other. You're in danger here. We need to help each other. You have to understand—"

Resentment snuck into my heart and hardened, crystallized into rage. "What I understand is that now I have two crazy parents. One was more than enough. One was more than I could manage. Do you understand that? Do you understand what you put me through when you were sane? And now you want to lose your mind? No."

I shouted so loud I fried my vocal cords.

My father's expression crumpled. His bottom lip quivered as he struggled to reply. He removed his glasses and pressed his palms against his eyes. He needed my help, and I shunned him. The image of his crestfallen face haunts me still.

Our neighbour hurried out into their yard to see who was causing the commotion. I could see the surprise on her face that for once it wasn't my mother.

I thought about all the times my dad left me alone in the house with her. Nights when she terrified me with her ranting, screaming like a soul possessed by a demon while she took a hammer to the mirrored cabinet in the upstairs bathroom. The times I hid in the closet and under the bed while she roamed the hallway threatening to torch the place with me in it.

I turned my back on him and stormed inside.

We spent the next days circling the subject whenever my

mother went to Mass. My father urged me to pay closer attention and begged that I be extra cautious in my dealings with
people. I couldn't know when I might encounter malevolence,
since many evil people adeptly shielded their true nature.

"Tu ne capisce. You don't understand. Some people live to
make other people suffer. People who make you see the moon's
reflection in water and make you think it's really the moon in
night sky. You'll drown before you realize who you're dealing
with. People like your mother love to destroy everyone around
them."

I was slow to fathom that my father had been quietly battling a delusional state before experiencing a complete breakdown. Even my mother—an acutely deranged woman—had
avoided the psych ward.

The twelve days of my trip spanned an eternity. One
night, after another failed attempt to talk to me about curs-
es and people filled with malevolent intent, my father paced
the upstairs hallway all night. My nervous system buzzed
with worry. I'd hear him muttering to himself, and then he'd
stop, open the door to my room and call my name, checking to see that I still existed. At midnight. At one, then two,
then two-thirty in the morning. At three, during a pause in
the pacing when my father went downstairs, I moved mom
into my room so she could lock the door. We were both still
awake, anticipating the worst. I took the spare bedroom
across the hall. He returned half an hour later, and when he
found my door locked, he banged on it.

I sat up and called out, "Papa, stop. Please go to bed. Can't
you see what you're doing?"

He looked in and didn't recognize me. "What are you doing
there? Who's in your room?"

"Mom is. Papa—"

He shrieked, calling on God and Femia to help. "Dio, aiutami. Mamma, aiutami. I'm supposed to be better. I wanted to be better for Eufemia's visit."

I scrambled to untangle myself from the bedsheets while he hollered. He repeated his cry for guidance like a mantra, bellowing at the ceiling. I reached him and put my hand on his arm, hoping to transmit calm.

I thought: please, please, please, please, please, please, please, please, please, please God, you deaf bastard, don't take my father. He's all I have.

My mother sprinted into the hallway. "Ma va fanculo, disgraziato—"

I wedged myself in the space between them, and we crashed, my mother's head knocking into my nose. I barely felt the sting. They hammered each other, kicking and slugging from side to side, trying to avoid me.

"Get out of the way, imbecile. This doesn't concern you. This is about me and your father—"

I pounded on her chest to push her back, but my mother enraged contained the strength of five boozed and ornery strapping young men looking for a fight to thrash their anguish into another soul.

My father kept lunging at her from the side. I shored against his efforts with my elbow, jabbing it repeatedly behind me into his ribs.

She punched past me to wallop my father. She screamed. "Who's the sick one now? It's you, it was always you. I married a crazy man."

I slapped her hard across the temple. "Shut up. This is all your doing. Congratulations, you drove someone crazy."

"So it's only me you have a problem with. You can't hear his insanity."

"Shut your fucking mouth. I swear to God, you shut the fuck up, or I'll shut you up forever, understand?"

How would I explain matricide to the police? No doubt, the phone book-sized file they had on my mother—the constant shoplifting, the assault charge from the onsite nurse at dad's factory, the restraining order issued to keep Aunt Sofia safe—could provide context. Maybe even a motive. Perhaps, after I committed the homicide I could pen a poignant suicide note:

Dear Toronto's Finest,
I stuck a fork in my mother because she was done. Then I offed myself. In all honesty, this madness is bullshit. While I fantasized about the potential decades spent in prison serving as a well-deserved writing retreat, I'm plum tuckered out.
Best regards,
Eufemia

They fought and they fought and they fought; sunlight broke through the living room window when I finally crumpled into a heap on my bed and fell into a dreamless sleep.

From the tranquil distance of time and therapeutic intervention, I can re-examine this dreadful scene. Watching my father come unhinged and my mother's cruel delight. How the last lines of Eliot's "The Hollow Men"—This is the way the world ends—played on a recorded loop in a corner of my brain that used words and sentences as life rafts. Fragments are written in a journal, but I failed to note how I managed to settle them down before dawn. My memory ends with my father trying to gift me the engraved watch he'd received for twenty-five years of service at his factory. He pressed it into my hands, rambling about not having a will and wondering what would happen to me when my mom finished him off.

Toward the end of the trip, my dad stated plainly that I was selfish and spoiled to stay away from home when he direly needed me. "You had a roof over your head and food on the table. What do you know of suffering?"

I knew exhaustion. I was intimate with fear. I perceived that I lived in British Columbia on borrowed time, borrowed money. Funds I never intended to pay back. The bank vault of transgressions brimming with support I thought my father owed me.

The day before my flight back to Victoria, he told me I would have to live with his death on my conscience.

His health crisis turned out to be diabetes. Unchecked, the disease can cause delirium. He was also diagnosed with severe depression, anxiety and obsessive-compulsive disorder My dad's doctor prescribed various meds to treat blood sugar levels and high blood pressure. It took thirteen pills a day to stabilize my father's mental and physical state.

It took forever to dawn on me that his grasp on reality was broken, had changed. For years as a teenager, as I observed the toll my mother's violence had on us both, I thought all the confusion lay in a combination of language barrier and cultural clash. My mother's schizophrenia acted as a solar eclipse, blocking my father's potential for illness.

On the other side of the country, in Victoria, I held myself together with paper clips and potato chips, writing and stuffing my face with junk food. The method, unscientifically proven to produce results, worked for awhile. But there came a day when I couldn't focus. Months, really. Words abandoned me— scattering like dandelion seeds in the breeze—or I left them. Unable to concentrate, I stopped attending classes and resigned myself to undergrad dropout status. The medication I took for atypical depression shaved fifteen pounds off my slender frame. Compliments poured in. The same pill wiped out my libido and drove a stake in the heart of my relationship. Kevin was from Cobble Hill—an island boy through and through, he loved a fun party, good company and me. We were attached at the groin for four years, loving and hurting each other, before meandering apart like driftwood. In our fifth and final year, our friends thought we'd already broken up because we spent so little time together.

Overtaxed by constant anxiety, I broke many bonds. The small circle of friends I'd managed to acquire shrunk. When I broke up with Kevin, it disappeared entirely. Our connection was in its death throes when another suitor came along. I basked in the glow of his attention and felt buffeted from the lonely sound of my heart pounding loudly late at night, sleep evading me as I attempted to suss out what would become of me.

It was a time of endings, of suspended animation, of shelved dreams and sluggish days spent nursing ancient hurts and numbing old aches. Time and distance healed nothing, as far as I could tell—this stint simply collected adversities and obstacles that distracted me for a stretch.

We cemented the deal: we moved to Vancouver and a couple of years later, I married the suitor. I was twenty-seven and thrilled that I'd never have to go on a date again. Bridal magazines didn't cover colour schemes that paired autumn weddings with existential dread. I chose my favourite colour for the two bridesmaids' dresses and the décor: eggplant purple. Our wedding took place on the day of Princess Diana's funeral. Fifty guests attended, including my dad, Rocco and Colleen. My father flew in on the pretence of a vacation — I couldn't tell my mother, couldn't risk the event being ruined. We had a short honeymoon on Bowen Island followed by monthly arguments about money that drained any affection between us. ogether for five years in total, the marriage lasted one revolution around the sun.

My father was relieved when the union ended. "I was worry for you. He no like to work. How can you plan the future with someone so lazy?"

"You should talk. How can you live with someone so crazy?"

"I want for your life to be easier."

"I wish the same. For you."

Temperance
(XIV)

She makes a commitment again.

Fifteen years after high school, I made my second tour of theatrical Thebes when my next newlywed husband mounted a production in February 2002. The difference between an eighteen-year old Theban chorus member and one of thirty-three? Stiffer joints. Thank Zeus, Greek tragedies don't call for big choreographed dance routines. Box office sales proved that a damp Vancouver winter matched with Sophocles' masterpiece on destiny and prophecy flirted with bankruptcy.

By then, I presumed no one could escape their fate.

A tarot reader I consulted for career advice had predicted this dicey second marriage following quick on the heel of a tumultuous first.

When she turned over the Tower card, I bit the inside of my lip and tasted blood. Until that moment, outside of my splitsville heartaches, my life away from home had been a streak of smooth-ish kismet. The card rarely appeared. The first time it did was when I was sixteen. I purchased a kit at the mall and used the book to analyze my self-readings before persuading my dad to sit for a Celtic Cross interpretation.

He relented, saying, "You believe in this outlandish stuff? So did your grandfather. And your grandfather's uncle. A blind soothsayer came to the village and told Nonno Gennaro's zio that he'd touch iron before his next birthday. Then he went to prison for killing a man who was bothering his sister."

"What? How many murderers are there in our family? Wait, don't answer. I need to concentrate."

I shuffled the deck and cut it into three piles, asking my dad to choose one. I didn't think to document the layout, the bulk of the meanings, the suits that came up, all of the spread is gone from memory but for the final outcome: the card of intense adversity and upheaval. The image amused him—two people tumbling headfirst out of a turret hit by lightning and enflamed.

"Doesn't look so good."

I paged through the guide. "It means things will get worse before they get better."

My reader said, "Don't panic, but be wary of the obstacles ahead." A few cards more: "Someone's going to show up in nine months, and you will need to scrutinize his relationship with his mother."

The following year, I ran into Tim, an acquaintance from Victoria's theatre scene, in town working on a show at the Playhouse Theatre. I had a crush on him, though with his blue eyes and chiselled features, he was rarely single for very long. He invited me over for dinner.

I sweated over the choice of outfit and then dressed casual in a flannel shirt and jeans, reminding myself that we were friends; this wasn't a mutual attraction.

He made a savoury coconut curry with Jasmine rice, and offered three different movie rentals to choose from. At 2 AM, after watching *Three Days of the Condor* and part of a *Mystery Science Theatre 3000*, I stood up to leave.

"You could crash here, if you like."

I gave him a puzzled look.

He talked me out of ordering a taxi, insisting he would walk me home. This seemed unnecessary, but I didn't clue in to his interest. The closer we got to my apartment, a short distance away, the tenser and terser he became. The moon loomed large and appeared close to earth.

I paused to admire the glow. "Wow. Look, it's almost full. What's a three-quarter moon called?"

"Ah. A three-quarter moon." Snarky tone.

An uncomfortable silence ensued.

At my door, I thanked him. He asked if we could keep talking, though we had walked in silence for the last ten minutes. I bit my tongue and invited him inside.

"I like you," he said. "But I'm here for a month. I don't know what this could lead to. Maybe nothing."

"We could enjoy the month, then." I wasn't looking for drama or complications, but his attention flattered me.

His shoulders relaxed, and he gave me a hug.

In the span of four weeks, we spent as much time together as possible. We stayed up late, discussing dreams and goals. Tim wanted to build a repertory company, similar to one he'd created in Victoria. He outlined play readings to organize and planned a list of shows to produce. A talented actor and director, his energy was infectious. We went for hour-long walks, talked about our favourite science fiction characters and shared our joy of kitschy Star Trek toys.

At night, back at my apartment, we dozed off pressed to-gether. As I listened to the rhythm of his breath and felt him drift off, his closeness soothed me into a deep, calming sleep.

Before the month ended, Tim dangled the bait of commit-ment, and I bit despite crimson flags waving in my peripheral vision. I noticed that he paid for everything with plastic and that his wallet never contained cash, but determined to en-joy myself, I willingly ignored the warning signs. Marinated in chaos, I barely blinked when trouble brewed—nothing and no one could be worse than what I'd grown accustomed to as a girl. I could handle a little financial stress. After six months apart, while he worked at a theatre festival in Southern Ontario, he moved back to Vancouver, broke and jobless, to be with me.

Tim threw a fit when I suggested that perhaps we could live in the same city without living together, arguing, "We're either together or we're not."

My casual attitude of "let's see where this might lead" dis-solved, fast. I went from confident to clingy in no time at all. I told myself this was how it was with creative types: passionate, and fuelled with fist-pounding-on-tables-type arguments. But this time, it would be different; this time, I would make things work while Tim got settled, found a job and pursued his acting ambition.

In our first six months living together, we moved twice in search of cheaper rent.

We regularly ate take-out Chinese, charging the food to my credit card. My debt and my waistline expanded.

Seven months after moving in with me, a few days after I'd

mused aloud about getting an apartment on my own, Tim proposed. I accepted. I was thirty-one.

A year into the marriage, my tension levels hit a tipping point that sent me back to therapy; since leaving Toronto and Dr. Salima's care, I had made my way to four other therapists' offices, each time hoping it would be the last. After the free-sessions failure from university, I found my way onto couches in several offices of therapists who specialized in co-dependency issues, depression or basic talk therapy. Even a regression therapist whose capstone session involved viewing traumatic events as a video, hitting pause, rewind, record and changing the event by envisioning a different course of action with a different outcome.

On my fifth attempt to fix myself, I saw Linda, an EMDR specialist. She suggested that Tim accompany me to an appointment. In six months, I had experienced two episodes of strep throat. I needed to practice better self-care.

During the hour-long appointment, two noticeable issues emerged: my consistent anger with Tim and his active avoidance of my company. Outside of arguing about it, Tim refused to discuss money. Every request I made to enlist his father's help in drawing up a budget—Tim's dad was an accountant—was flatly dismissed.

Linda laid down ground rules. "When she swears at you during an argument, you leave. Let her sit with her own actions. You don't have to make her feel better. That's not behaviour that should be tolerated."

"That doesn't seem right. Who leaves in the middle of an argument?"

"I'm saying if it becomes verbally abusive, like you've both said it has, then you walk away. You can discuss it when cooler heads prevail."

Tim remained sceptical.

"Now, what about setting aside time in your schedule to do something together. Can you agree to do something, maybe an hour a week, every week?"

He scoffed. "Of course I can."

My right eye twitched. I put my hand up to stop the spasm. "Then why haven't we?"

The truth was no one could help us. In terms of affection, budgets, and responsibilities, we spoke completely different languages.

THE DEVIL.

The Devil

(XV)

She obsesses.

F or years I delivered the same joke: "My mother's name is Lucy, short for Lucifer." The quip doesn't play with Italian crowds. Mothers are revered as paragons of virtue, patience and love in the Bel Paese. A popular southern saying is "La mamma è sempre la mamma:" Mother will always be mother. I envied the simpleton with a proud, doting mom who created the hackneyed phrase.

In every anecdote I told about my mother, she was the villain, yet in truth, she was a victim. During that awful summer we spent in Bonefro, Nonno Barone had taken my dad aside to suggest an honour killing. He recommended his son-in-law locate a doctor who could administer a needle that would put my mother to sleep for good, as if his daughter was a rabid dog instead of a woman in agony—diseased, furious and afraid.

My father shared the news of Barone's callous proposition with me the sticky summer I turned seventeen, one evening while I sat on the veranda smarting from another dustup. He called Barone an ignorant peasant. Numb and weary, I disagreed: no, worse than ignorance was his malevolence.

With my second marriage failing, I saw my mother everywhere. In the 6'2" homeless black man who hung out on the corner near the Skytrain station. Once, he narrowly missed punching me in the head. Agitated, he yelled, "I don't give a fuck, your mother's a fucking crasher." It was all so quick—just beyond my sightline—I didn't flinch. I felt the closeness of his fist, the short distance and air between his hand and the side of my head, the space behind my ear. Most people would cross the street to avoid walking past him. I made no eye contact but continued on, business as usual. This subtle Buddhist act of kindness, to walk close to his suffering, and repeat a mantra to ease his affliction. I saw my 5' mother in him, in the way he raged.

I saw her in the woman with the drugstore carrot-coloured hair crossing the street in front of my building on her way to the supermarket, her expression frozen in a permanent frown, extreme and almost cartoonish, as if she were smelling sewage everywhere. She had a belly that jutted out, pronounced because she carried herself in a posture that kept her shoulders squared and back straight. She marched out in front of the traffic in a determined step, expecting drivers to slow. She even dressed like my mother in overly tight capri pants, wedge heels and a top with embroidered bits, beads and sequins.

An older fellow walked into one of the independent grocers in my Commercial Drive hood while I picked out the best package of raspberries. He came in, hands stuffed in the pockets of his light jacket, looking uncomfortable. His shoulders hunched, he had a slim build. He asked to speak to the manager while I stood in line behind him, waiting to pay. He asked for a job, and the manager told him to bring in a resume. I saw my mother in the way the man asked, his accent, and his posture.

I got angry then, sweated with the desire to say something, knowing it wasn't my place, that my speaking out wouldn't land the man a job. Ask him to give you references, give him a trial period, check his body fat content and ability to lift heavy loads—but a resume to stock watermelons? I collected my change and pushed my way past people, out of the store. I was crying by the time I got home, five blocks away, because the scene at the grocers reminded me of a conversation with my mother. She went from corner store to convenience store in her neighbourhood, asking for a job, and everyone told her they needed a recipe. She didn't understand, she wasn't asking to work as a cook.

I said, "Resume. It's called a resume."

The elderly white-haired balding woman carefully counting out her pennies, holding up the express line, she's like my mother too. My mother held up lines at Towers, demanding that the cashier accept and cash her baby bonus cheques even when she'd forgotten to bring appropriate ID. She wouldn't budge until she got her way. People behind us would grumble. The cashier would start out fine and grow astonished by my mother's belligerence. The cashier would look at me; I would look down at my feet. The manager would come, and extra cashiers to deal with the backed-up line. She would draw a crowd, not care if others had to suffer through her unreasonable requests. It's in the deliberation.

The homeless man having an animated conversation with the air, who I followed down the street because he happened to say, "I'm not mother," as I neared him on the sidewalk. I stopped at a storefront and pretended to be window-shopping. He wore work pants the same green shade sanitation workers wear, and a heavy winter coat, in the middle of a July heat wave. He stopped and made a comment every time someone walked by; I saw my mother in the level of his illness.

The emaciated woman dealing with an addiction issue — I kept running into her on the corner outside my work. I saw my mother in her lack of spatial boundaries.

The guy asking for change outside the liquor store: in his degree of need.

Once, sitting in a Tim Hortons with my father, I watched a woman unload the groceries from her cart into the trunk of her car. The movements of her mouth mesmerized me, they formed a series of involuntary grimaces; I guessed that she had no teeth for her entire face to rearrange so intensely in the quick and jerky motions, similar to those unconscious movements my mom would make. I wondered if she had tardive dyskinesia, a neurological disorder that is often a side effect of antipsychotic drugs. The lack of muscle control, the automatic spastic actions, are a couple of the most visible aspects of a lengthy, chronic illness like schizophrenia; they signal that a serious brain disorder has taken root in the mind like a vine choking out logic and perception. I saw my mother in the woman's unconscious tics.

I saw her everywhere I lived. In some manner, I was always looking for her, the same way she always searched for me.

The Tower
(XVI)

She experiences sudden
upheaval—afresh.

Late January of 2004, we arrived home past midnight from a fundraising event for Tim's theatre company to find that my mother had called multiple times. I listened to the first voicemail and decided to wait until morning to deal with the rest. I turned the ringer off, and we went to bed. In the morning, I listened to message after message of her frustrated sighs and snide tone in Italian: "Why aren't you home? Where the hell are you at this time of night? Do you hear me? Are you not answering because it's me?" Finally, on the last she said, "Call home, Papa go hospital."

My heart did a frenzied dance while I waited for someone to pick up. No one answered.

I phoned Aunt Angelina—another no answer.

Finally, I reached my Aunt Sofia. My father was in emergency at Trillium Hospital.

Dad had called her, distressed, his voice strained: he couldn't take the burden, couldn't carry his cross to bear any longer. He'd made too many mistakes. He had taken all his sleeping pills and called 911 but was drowsy and losing focus. Alarmed, seventy-year-old Sofia bolted out of her home wearing a cardigan and her slippers. The sidewalks were salted and uneven. She navigated the patches of ice as quickly as she could, arriving at her brother's home as the paramedics were leaving: the house appeared empty. My mother had locked and bolted the door—refusing to respond. In Sofia's best English, she pleaded with the young men to break down the door. Her brother was inside, dying. The medics knocked louder. The lock rattled. Mom answered, annoyed at the disturbance. She held crochet hooks and a doily project.

The paramedics found my father slumped between the wall and his bed. They checked his vitals, administered first aid and carried him out on a stretcher for transport to the nearest hospital.

I sat on the floor, half-collapsing, cross-legged, and sobbed. My legs shook. I wheezed like I'd run up a flight of stairs. "What? N'age capite. Can you repeat—I don't understand."

"Is bad. How he can think to do this? Last night. His voice. I knew something was wrong. He didn't sound right. I say to him phone ambulance."

My mind raced faster than my heartbeat, all manner of jumbled clichéd thoughts passed through: this was the price of freedom. Everything came at a cost, the pound of flesh closest to your heart. I bent over and keened. Not this again. Not this purgatory. Fourteen years after my father's first all-consuming battle with psychosis, I felt the same grief-steeped guilt.

I interrupted my aunt: "This is my fault."

"No say that." My aunt gave me the hospital's number, waiting while I crawled to my desk, found a pen and returned to the phone.

We said goodbye, and I paced the living room, back and forth. Like my father. He never sat still for long. Life with my mother made him a moving target, always on his feet, on the go, heading out the door. Now his life, the tapestry woven through the time of our shared history, the thread that was him, was in danger of being cut.

I contained an equal measure of rage and grief. I felt my heart could go supernova like a sun in a secluded galaxy and shroud my world in darkness.

When I called the hospital and reached patient inquiry, I told them my father's name.

"Michelantonio Fantetti. Michael Anthony Fantetti, but it's a complete name in Italian. He goes by Mike but some people call him Tony."

The nurse couldn't locate him.

"Is this Trillium? In Mississauga?" I wanted to tell her he answers to the name Papa. I wanted to ask if she could put me on the speaker system. He'd answer if he heard my voice.

"What's he here for?"

"Attempted suicide."

With no change in her professional tone, she said, "One moment please." Sixty long seconds later, she came on the line again. He was still in emerge. "They're getting him a bed. You'll have to call back later."

A mantra of indignation repeated itself.

How could he do this?

Why would he do this?

How could he do this to me?

I searched for someone other than myself to blame. His doctor. My mother. Himself. His cultural background. His faith that the hand of God would intervene. The Catholic Church.

I finally got through to my dad that afternoon. My aunt said his voice had been flat, monotonous for a month. I could hear nothing but terror when he spoke.

"Be careful. Everywhere you go, watch out. Mamma—"

The narrative I had repressed except as a punch line cascaded out in his frenetic speech: my mother was possessed. She was evil incarnate. She'd been sent by the devil to destroy us. Thank God I lived so far away. The distance made it harder for her to do her demonic handiwork. From the hospital phone at the nurse's station, he whispered the story to me as quietly as possible, so that my mother wouldn't hear him with what he imagined to be her bionic Beelzebub ability. He said she'd been paying sorcerers skilled in nefarious arts to murder him.

For years my mother wandered through the house, bitter and laying siege, shouting, "I'll be widowed before I ever divorce this piece of garbage." I thought my father's ears were plugged with cotton. I couldn't fathom how he withstood the menace. He hadn't. This was him, cracking under the burden of her wicked temper.

The past echoed into the present. Once again, he begged me to come home and be with him. Once again, I failed the hero test.

All my life I felt as though my father had been waiting for me to fix the unsolvable mess that was this gnarled, acrimonious union. Behind his repeated statements that "Everything would be taken care of" and that he had "everything under control," existed a complicated formula with a complex solution to the twisted situation that I alone was meant to discover, and implement. The simplest equation—the one I grew up with, two against one—was likely the resolution he hoped for.

He waited for my answer.

I said no. I couldn't.

An old sermon resurfaced. The one about me being selfish and spoiled. How he'd done nothing but support me. He added new lines to the soliloquy: I'd been nothing but a drain on him, a parasite, like everyone else.

"If I'm not alive tomorrow, your mother finished me off. And you didn't come to say goodbye. That's on you for the rest of your life." He hung up.

I stared at the phone. The dial tone buzzed.

Five minutes later, Rocco called.

I answered, high-pitched and hysterical and incomprehensible.

"Listen to me, you can't fix this situation. You understand me? This is not your mess."

Rocco stayed on the phone with me while I wailed. When I calmed down, he told me to drink water and go for a walk.

"Are you kidding? I don't want to go outside."

"What you want to do? Stay inside and cry? That's not going to help."

"It can't hurt."

After a few days, my father camouflaged his distress. The hospital gave him a weekend pass. He would leave and finish what he started. He calmly said goodbye, and told me he was sorry to learn of my true nature: ingrate.

I called back to speak to the nurse but bungled my words, bawling and begging her to cancel the pass.

Tim rushed into the room and grabbed the phone. "Listen, my wife is understandably upset right now so you can talk to me. You need to understand. You can't let him out. My father-in-law is still threatening to kill himself. That's what he's saying to his daughter."

The nurse expressed surprise: My father was projecting a serene façade to the staff because he wanted out. They cancelled his pass.

I finally connected with the hospital's social worker the next day. She recommended shock treatment. "He's not getting better on the meds, and we all feel it's unfair to let him suffer like this."

She asked if I had power of attorney, if I could make decisions on my father's behalf.

"No. I don't." I let her know that fourteen years prior, during his first and only psychotic break before this one, his medications were tweaked enough to save his life. I never prepared for another crisis. Stupid. Stupid. Stupid.

Meds stopped working sometimes, she said. She would try to convince him to undergo the treatment. "Forget what you've heard about this from Hollywood or bad movies. The results have been life-altering for patients."

The next time I called and spoke with him, he asked me what I thought about "electricity shock." Full of fear and doubt, he said, "Something has to be done, I no can go on like this."

My heart broke so many times that winter, I lost count. I thought nothing could ever make me smile or laugh again. I curled up in bed and got through the months of February and March by sleeping and going to work. I barely noticed Tim's upcoming theatre project. His decision to mount the play came after my father was committed to the psych ward and kept him away until late at night—he usually returned after I'd fallen fitfully asleep. Some nights he found me in bed staring at the ceiling. He talked about rehearsals, production notes, anything to distract me, but my mind acted like a sieve. I retained nothing, incapable of following or maintaining a conversation.

The hospital recommended up to ten to twelve electroshock treatments for my father.

"You think is safety?"

"I think it will help, Papa. I heard it helps a lot of people with severe depression."

He wasn't convinced, but he went through with the treatment. Humbled, I saw that I had confused his indecision and deep kindness for fear. I understood nothing. He provided an example of indestructible courage and bottomless compassion. I had been resentful for too long that he hadn't saved me from my mother's deranged assaults. One man against the weight of tradition and expectation fending off a woman with a treatment-resistant strain of schizophrenia—no wonder his health buckled. After his sixth treatment, I reached him on the hospital line.

When I heard the elation in his voice at hearing from me, I realised how seldom I'd heard him joyful. "I feel better. Thank you for calling me. Chickpea. You're the one good thing I did with my life."

Hearing my childhood nickname made my voice catch. I blinked back tears. "That's not true. You're the good thing you've done with your life."

"I was lose my way, but everything going to be better now. Don't you worry."

I almost cracked a joke: Who, me? Why would I worry? I slumped, leaning back on the couch. Took a breath and relaxed my shoulders on a slow exhale.

"Ti voglio bene, Papa. Tante, tu ne sai quande." He couldn't know how much I loved him. Because I kept my distance, this time and last, every time he needed me, each time he clung to life by a fist. I thought of Nonno Gennaro's vices and his inability to appreciate this decent, hard-working son. I considered Grandfather Baron's soulless suggestion to have his daughter put down like a lame beast of burden. The poverty and harsh conditions that created them also produced my dad.

"I know I'm lucky to have you as my father."

"Okay," he said. I could hear the smile in his upbeat tone. "Let's we say I was good for you and you was good for me. Okay?"

"Okay." I hung up the phone and bawled.

Two weeks after the conversation with my father on the mend, I hit a point of impenetrable frustration in the cycle of mounting unpaid bills with Tim.

Linda, my therapist, said, "You don't have to pay people to love you."

I sat back in the chair with the weight of her words pressing my chest, squeezing my heart. I put my hand on my collarbone and rubbed the area below it. I massaged the space above my chest, the place yoga practitioners say houses the heart chakra: it felt sore and painful. I might have had reflux. I bent over and put my head between my knees, trying to slow my breath.

"Will you be all right?"

I gave a muffled affirmative reply as I tried to quell the rising nausea.

"You don't have to buy anyone's loyalty. You're worthy."

"Uh huh." I held my head in my hands.

I made plans to move out. I asked Tim to manage his own

expenses for six months. I wanted a break from paying for groceries, rent, hydro, and phone plus internet while he extended his maxed-out credit cards, digging trenches of enormous debt to produce another Jacobean tragedy for the discerning theatregoer.

"You walk out that door, our marriage is over."

"Then I guess we never really had one." After all the hyped-up festivities had ended—the party, the gown, the wedding guests—we had a feast-or-famine relationship: I footed the bill and still felt starved for affection. A husband who spouted Shakespeare now repeated vapid movie-of-the-week script lines?

My parents' marriage was finally over, and four months later—during the Transit of Venus when the planet of love passed in front of the summer sun—so was mine.

The Star

(XVII)

*She engages in wishful thinking,
catastrophizing and
self-fulfilling prophecies.*

My father had decided if he survived another plummet into despair, he would never again set foot in the house he had called home for thirty-six years. He promised himself in the ambulance on the way to the hospital to give up everything—including the home he worked so hard to earn—to gain stability.

He returned once to the house with a social worker's assistance to collect his Bible and keepsakes: old photos and documents.

He'd been away five months. Mayhem greeted him inside. My mother had done the work of a wrecking crew. The tiled kitchen floor, upstairs and downstairs, cracked and chipped, in parts demolished beyond repair. The glass from the good stove had been shattered; it lay strewn inside the oven. Holes dotted the walls, the plaster crumbling into dust. A window in the basement was broken. Leaves, twigs and dirt littered the space below.

He returned to his tiny bachelor apartment and flipped through his cherished book in search of his favourite passages. Only jagged edges remained from the ripped-out pages.

"The house is gone, Chickpea. She destroyed the value. She ruined the furniture too. The couch had stuffing coming out. Looked like it had been attacked with scissors. I can't believe the house is gone."

"But you're still here. That's worth more."

My mother believed she could make the house unsaleable and force my father to come back. Instead, she knocked $300,000 off the asking price, and it sold for a song—a funeral dirge.

Six years later, my father's colectomy surgery—a routine procedure—was beset by complications and required a life-saving blood transfusion. The signs were clear: I moved back to Toronto in the summer of 2010. I developed a habit of constantly looking over my shoulder. Three times a week, I made the hour-long trek by subway and bus to see my father, passing through the familiar geography of those rough years.

On the bus, I passed nondescript houses and giant warehouse-sized stores, restaurants and strip malls. In winter, the route would be every possible shade of grey: slate, battleship, ash. The crushed glass in the concrete sidewalk is the one thing that sparkles there. Everything about the area feels hard, concrete and steel, and the small plots of front and backyard grass do nothing to make it seem less austere. The correctional centre, turned into a maximum security "super-prison," will house over a thousand inmates. Mimico Asylum was a college campus. My father lived within walking distance of the jail; my mother now lived across the street from the old mental hospital. She'd been moved back into the area by her social worker when an apartment became available in supportive housing.

Once, she wandered around the pastoral school grounds and looked into the buildings, searching for my father. She approached a campus security guard, asking if he had seen her husband.

She related the story over the phone. "He should be here," she said. "He's cuckoo."

"This is a school now," answered the guard. "They don't keep crazies here."

"Lascia perde, Ma. You're divorced now."

"I no ask for the divorce. I no want," she said, reverting to English.

Her rent-controlled apartment building was visible from the bus. I felt as if I tempted fate every time I trekked out to Etobicoke to see my dad: I didn't want to run into my mother.

I imagined three crones, all maternal ancestors, meddling in my affairs from the spirit realm: my great-grandmother Leonilda, my grandmother Sapooch and my mother. All three had a similar temperament, but only my mother still lived. She searched for me in the bushes that surrounded her apartment building. Other times she took transit to harangue my Aunt Sofia, or dropped in on another relation, insisting that the woman ran a brothel from her home, and that I was the busiest prostitute.

I pictured these fates asking each other if I should be spared their destinies: madness and maltreatment. Sometimes I would talk to the dead. No answer.

Over dinner with my dad, I told him about a recent conversation with my mother: I'd reconnected with her through the internet so she couldn't trace my local phone number. She had made a new friend, one who drove her to Mississauga, to my Aunt's Angelina's home. Too far to travel by transit, it spared her the pricey taxi fare. Instead, she sat in the car and watched, hoping to catch a glimpse of me.

I tried to stay calm when she described how no one knew the colour of the car or that she was in Mississauga. I pried details from her, but I felt like a python had wrapped itself around me, slowly squeezing the air out of my lungs: don't panic, don't shout, I told myself. But before I cut the call off, I threatened that I wouldn't visit and would stop calling for good.

"And you believed her?"

"Excuse me?"

"You think is true this story she told you?"

The temperature in my father's dingy pad was searing. Outside, in the July heat, the day missed being a record-breaker by one degree. The city of Toronto had issued a heat alert.

I glared at him.

The week before he had questioned whether I trusted another anecdote my mother told me about having a bank card. She knew her PIN but didn't understand what buttons to push on the machine. I couldn't understand how it was possible that a woman under the guardianship of the Public Trustee of Ontario with a specific weekly allowance would be given a bank card, unless the bank and her guardian didn't care if she went through her entire account, her $200,000 takeaway from their divorce, in six months. She was capable of burning through the money in less time, no doubt. That was exactly what would happen if she learned to withdraw cash beyond her weekly allowance.

"Non è vero. You believe?" My father thought I fell for every sob story my mother fed me, as if I was made of the same gullible, naïve stock he had demonstrated throughout my childhood. Three and a half decades as a battered husband, unable to make up his mind to divorce her, believing God would step in and fix our critical predicament while we skidded through crisis after disaster after catastrophe. My voice rose until I was yelling.

"Yes, I do. Because what, there is something so unbelievable about that? The story you think makes no sense is Mom finding someone in her building to give her a ride. Yeah that's wildly unbelievable! But no! She's skilled in dark arts magic, and a handmaiden of the devil—that's the truth?"

My father looked down at his plate of trout and shrugged. He'd stepped on a landmine. "There is no solution."

"There is always planning ahead to avoid trouble. You found a solution though it took you thirty-six years."

"That's right. I waited too long because I'm stupid."

My mother had berated my father their entire married life, and now I was carrying on in the same manner. My flight-or-fight instinct never switched off. Someone was constantly on the ropes—in this instance, my dad. I was bashing old bruises, so I backed down. "No. You weren't stupid. You were a little soft though."

"This is what I'm telling you. Don't be soft with her. Every time you talk with her it leaves you upset."

Waiting at the bus stop across from his apartment, I worried about getting home without being spotted. A car pulled up to drop someone off. I hunched my shoulders, peering sideways through my sunglasses to figure out if I should walk away. A man slid out of the passenger seat, and I relaxed. I said a quick thank-you to the fates; I hoped my Canadian politeness could tip the scales away from Southern Italian sacrifices.

And then it happened: with my father, on a brief excursion to pick up bread at No Frills Supermarket, a month after my return.

My father saw her first. "Oh boy. You know who here? Mamma."

I froze. "Where?"

We stood in the produce section, not far from the entrance. A bread run, the most basic errand, turned into a stock-the-fridge-and-cupboards affair because I was shopping with someone who'd survived the Second World War and the Italian Campaign.

My father handed me the basket, filled with cantaloupe, raspberries, bananas and two cans of chickpeas. "You take to the cash, I get the bread and meet you there."

I shook my head. "No, Papa. We're going, *now*."

"You right." My father took back the groceries and made for the express cashier. I followed meekly behind. No lineup, but I couldn't understand why my dad didn't have the same sense of urgency.

"Dad—"

"We shouldn't leave without the food—"

"I can't believe you." I faced away from the entrance, staring at the monitor that beeped scanned items: the noise quickened my pulse. My heart pounded, shuddering in my chest. I thought of the cliché—no sudden movements—praying that if I succeeded in being stealthy, we'd escape unnoticed. I turned as we left and chanced a glance.

My mother pushed an empty cart along the section of lettuce and vegetables, the area we'd deserted minutes prior. She'd gained a lot of weight, enough to be considered obese. She leaned over the cart with poor posture as she walked, ambling, using the buggy for support. Her hair frizzed with too much pouf: this indicated how unwell she was—a woman meticulous in keeping her monthly salon appointment. Dressed in complete black that must have been suffocating in the sweltering late-summer heat wave, she wore heels—she always wore heels—and lumbered forward. Her gait, her bearing, her aloneness, the intimate details of her essence drummed up an ancient yearning in me. A familiar heaviness swamped through my chest. My throat constricted.

Outside the supermarket, a blast of unrelenting heat hit us: 9:30 in the morning, and it was 29° Celsius with the potential for another spike, a scorcher for the record books. No breeze came from the nearby lake, a five-minute walk from this suburban cement paradise.

"I come here all ways, all the time, I never was see before—" Dad unlocked the passenger door and handed me the bags.

I darted in and buckled up. The parking lot, like the store, was enormous. Did she see us enter? She must have. We were inside for two minutes before my dad noticed her, and it would have taken at least that long for her to cross the lot from the street. I wished I could convince myself that she hadn't seen us. Wouldn't she have made a scene? Could she have learned restraint?

"Better I don't tell my sisters. They think I take too many risks."

"Should I say I told you so now, or do you want me to tell you later? How about I tell you every day for the rest of your life? Because I told you so. I told you so. You never listen—"

In the safety of the car, I hollered my dismay.

"You always take too many chances. Nothing has changed, and you've learned nothing. Take all the risks you want but leave me out of it. From now on, *fanculo*, go everywhere by yourself. I should never have come back here. For what? To feel like a terrified five-year-old because I went with you to get stupid bread for your fucking toast. I don't need this. I don't. Look at me, look, my hands, I can't stop shaking — "

"You're right."

Even after arriving back at his apartment building, we didn't get out of the car because I wouldn't stop ranting. I couldn't stop. Deep into my fury but not so far gone that I wanted to mortify him, alert neighbours or turn this safe home into a dungeon — I would not become my mother. No matter that her volcanic temperament coursed through me in anger or fear. I would never let anyone put me in jeopardy again. No, I would not become my mother, nor would I allow myself to be as meek as my father.

He sat, jingling his keys and nodding, until spent I burst into sobs.

For years, nothing would change in my mother's mental state or behaviour, but any time she remained lucid, I'd think: this is it, we've turned a corner. At some point, another crossroad, I realized I'd been thinking about corners like structured city blocks, not the random angles of swirling chaos present at the dawn of time, at the start of the universe, twirling out farther and farther, encompassing more space, time, energy and distance than I could comprehend. Every time I told someone about her — a therapist, a friend, a partner — the same dismal tale emerged. I made adjustments in the telling, considered the audience, but the basics would stay the same, our stuck saga of gloom. My parents and I, petrified like the people of Pompeii, caught forever in personal agony. Then I realized my assumptions were impossible: the underlying constant of existence is change. My mother was capable of adaptation. Her illness had transformed: it worsened. Psychosis was perdition.

That evening, I Skyped my mother.

She answered on the first ring. "I saw you with Papa today. You live here now. Everyone told me you moved back to Toronto. And I said my daughter would tell me. She's a good girl."

"Non è vero. Chi t'ha ditte?"

"Tutte quande."

"No, sono i voce. You can't listen to the voices. They aren't telling you the truth." My stomach ached as I churned out lies. "Papa was sick. I came to help. I didn't want to say anything. He doesn't want to see you."

"Allora? M'anche tu me vi trouva?"

The yearning in her request unravels my plans. I promised to visit the following week, pretending to extend a return flight to Vancouver. I felt the pretzel-shaped knot in my gut tighten.

"You'll stay with me."

"Una notte—"

"Una? All this times you stay with you father and for me, your Mamma, one night?"

"I'm not staying with Dad. I'm staying at a friend's. One night or no night, it's up to you."

My mind looped the track: what if, what if... I'd have to turn my cell phone off. Better yet, leave it behind so she didn't see the Toronto area code. But what if there was an emergency and I couldn't reach the landline, or what if she cut the wire? What if it were my destiny to be murdered by my mother? The more I tried to block out dread, the stronger it advanced:

What if it were my destiny to be murdered by my mother?

What if it were my destiny to be murdered by my mother?

A couple of hours after yelling at my dad, I mentally negotiated the possible end for this cycle of suffering: fine, I could be scrappy. I wouldn't go down without a fight.

She sighed. She'd taken her pills but hadn't received her monthly injection yet. She asked questions about the friend I was purportedly staying with: Who was this person? Where did they live? How did I meet them? Were they Italian?

I deflected. "None of this matters, Mamma. I can stay one night, and I'll visit for a couple of days before I head home."

In her exhaustion, she capitulated.

We would do it my way. The slapdash plan felt fraught with potential errors: I was bound to slip up in a simple way. I would make a purchase in her presence and expose the new library card in my wallet. A receipt could fall out of my purse. She'd rustle through my Day-Timer when I went to the bathroom and find local phone numbers. Trying to outwit a woman who had excellent antennae for altered details even when she was medicated leached all my stamina.

"Where is Papa?"

"Ma, ferme. I can't tell you."

Six years since my father had left with a paramedic escort, and my mother still believed he'd return repentant. She would take him back, of course, and give him grief for this truancy.

"When is your father going to stop being an idiot? I'm tired of holding the sign of the horns." The implication in this old-world expression: My father was unfaithful, carrying on affairs while she, the dutiful wife, warded off the evil eye of his shameful behaviour with a hand gesture.

"You're divorced."

She shrieked. "I didn't sign papers!"

My mother's yelling elicited a tendon-hammer-on-the-knee-joint reaction from me, but I kept calm. "Lower your voice or I'm hanging up. You didn't have to sign papers."

The lawyer my father retained said he'd never dealt with anyone as arduous in his thirty years of practice. The drawn-out case took four years to conclude.

"I'm Catholic. I am not divorced. Your father is married to me. He's my husband. Who is the whore he took up with? When I catch her—"

A streetcar whirred past my apartment and chimed the warning bell for jay-walking pedestrians. I ran to close every window before another sound could betray location.

"—If you coming, you stay, no going back Vancouver. Finish this life coming and going. Mamma need you."

"—No, Ma. I'm sorry. That's not possible."

When I left Toronto at nineteen, the scuttlebutt among some paesani was that I'd abandoned an ill mother and a frazzled father. Deprived them of a translator and a safeguard. The complexity of my mother's disease was beyond debate, but that didn't deter people from offering pointless, well-meaning advice: There is nothing to be done. Everyone has crosses to bear. The Book of Destiny has already been written.

The problem with predestination: People are absolved of their responsibility. Inaction rules the day, the week, the months, the years.

In my final weeks out west, I stopped at the small table and stool set up in a doorway on Commercial Drive to get a reading from a man I'd walked by for years. I pulled out my notebook and asked permission to record the session. As he shuffled his

Tarot deck, I concentrated on focusing my telepathic powers into my questions: "Is this move a dreadful idea? Is this change going to be strenuous? How difficult on a scale of DEFCON 1 to 5? Am I going to regret this? How much on a device that gauges Richter magnitude levels? Should I tell my mother I was moving back to Toronto?"

He laid the Celtic Cross out before me; the Page of Swords appeared first. Not this guy again. A court card that showed up all the time. Him or the Queen of Wands if I relaxed. I rarely relaxed. This young man with the wind-swept hair, brandishing a sword ready for battle, had followed me through readings for years. He was wary, cautious, curious and always looking behind him. In other words, he was me.

"The ground under your feet is moving and your head is in the clouds."

I told the reader this could describe me every day of my life. And that I was moving back to the city I was born in, that I'd fled, back to the city that surfaced in my nightmares. Tectonic plates shifted, the Earth spun on its axis, and I fumbled along, falling, dusting myself off and getting back up. When did I ever feel like I stood on solid ground? Never, that's when. Four cards from the Major Arcana appeared—the life-lessons-en-route-to-enlightenment cards, the archetypes accompanying souls on their journey. Death, The Lovers, The High Priestess and The Hermit meant change, choices, intuition and introspection. The suit most represented was swords: of course I thought about struggle and fight. The Hail Caesar gladiator-salute approach to life thrummed through my mind at a steady interval. Also in the cards were clarity, intellect and the quality of air—logic and the ability to reason.

The reader wore a pensive expression as he stared at the

cards, then at me.

I paused the note-taking and gave him a tentative grin. So what if two Major Arcana cards opposed each other and one depicted inexorable forces? I wanted to reassure him I was fine.

He didn't buy it. "Worrying won't fix anything, so stop worrying."

Please. Dogs bark. Cats meow. Fish swim. My people worry: we excel at getting in a tizzy. Vexation is hardwired into our DNA. I exhaled loudly and, with my inside voice, said goodbye to twenty bucks.

He looked over the cards again and back at me. "Knowledge is your fortune."

"I see. I wish money was my fortune."

He smiled. "There's an opportunity for healing here."

With all those swords? I thought I should batten down the hatches and prepare to face the coming storm: Hurricane Lucia, my mother. I thanked him for the reading and left figuring I'd also ask someone to assess the planetary configurations.

The astrologer I consulted told me more: "This move is the best decision you've made in a long time. It's fantastic. Get a naturopath, your energy is a bit sluggish. Drink green tea and quit using sugar. Your metabolism and two of your chakras are really out of whack. You're a little out of whack in general."

This wasn't news to me or anyone I'd met.

"My mother? Should I tell her?" So many years of talk therapy, so many conversations with healthcare providers, psychologists and psychiatrists and law enforcement, and I preferred a stargazer check my Jupiter, my Saturn, my rising sign, the retrogrades, something, anything that could help me. I knew what I wanted (no contact with my mother except over the phone), and someone needed to tell me what I wanted was permissible. Hell, it had to be acceptable.

"Leave her be. Nothing will quench her thirst. Take it up to the spirit level and talk to her spirit, not her. Send white light through prayer. Don't tell her."

I interrupted my mother's tirade on revenge. She planned to suss out the folks who had done our family damage and pulled us apart.

"Ma, I'll see you next Tuesday. We can go to your doctor together, okay? I'll come with you and keep you company."

"That's my problem. I don't have any company. I'm all alone here. I don't have schizophrenia. I have too much solitude. I'm lonely."

The Moon
(XVIII)

She listens to her intuition and battles illusions.

A night before my impromptu visit, my mother phoned the police in Vancouver, insisting that someone had broken into my home and attacked me. At two in the morning Pacific Time, they sent officers and an ambulance to the address I gave as my own—for mail and for insurance mom wouldn't discern my true whereabouts: my best friend Cathy's apartment in East Vancouver. The response team buzzed intercoms and made their way into the building: neighbours were woken up, the landlord was notified.

Cathy was on an overnight at her mum's. She let me know what had transpired as I locked the door behind me and made for the subway.

My heart sank with heaviness. Again. Again. Not this again. Again.

I'd made a list of errands to complete and take care of—

my mother wanted to find a job. I hoped to get her medication refilled and ensure the monthly needle was administered. I'd promise to help her fill out applications for jobs and volunteer positions if she agreed to go to the doctor with me. I needed to check her cupboards for alcohol and stock shelves with pasta, tins of tomato sauce, nuts or other sources of healthy protein. I crumpled the list and tossed it to the bottom of my backpack.

It was a Tuesday morning, cold, wet and grey. Perhaps it was an omen, this Vancouver sky above me. The damp enveloped me—I felt it in my bones.

My mother answered her intercom within seconds of my buzzing her number. "I was see you on the security TV."

She stood at the elevator as the doors opened on her floor. Grasping my forearm, she pulled me into a fierce hug, smothering me with kisses on both cheeks—five, six loud smooches. "Let me see my daughter. Daughter de mamma. So long I no see you. Too long I no see you."

I pulled away.

An elderly neighbour from across the hall opened her apartment door.

"This my daughter." My mother puffed up her chest with pride. "I telling you she was come for see me."

"Yes, you did." The neighbour, Mrs. Perkins, shook my hand. "She's been very excited about your visit, it's all she talks about."

"You want have coffee? I just was make."

Mrs. Perkins declined: in Italian my mother says, "Well thank goodness, what a nosy neighbour, coming to her door like that."

I smiled at Mrs. Perkins as we said goodbye and entered my mother's apartment.

She had a fantastic view of Lake Ontario and the Toronto skyline. Her one bedroom, situated on the twelfth floor, was spacious and roomy, with an empty closed-off balcony area: no plants, nor any of the usual knick-knacks she collected from dollar stores. Knockoff ceramic cherubs sat on the television stand. Assorted furnishings, the grandfather clock, the baroque coffee table, the dining room set and 10,000 crocheted doilies she'd managed to retrieve from the house. She lived in stark contrast to my father in his pint-sized bachelor apartment above a print shop. Her building also had an amenities room, a care-taker, and a thoroughly modern security system: She'd watched me approach the building. Four cameras monitored the various entrances and common areas of the building. She had a safe home, yet she heard voices of murderers in the walls.

She set coffee on the table with espresso cups, a matching sugar bowl and creamer.

"When your plane was land?"

"What do you mean? I've been here already for a week. You saw me, remember?"

"I went to the airport. I didn't see you. I watched all the people, the ones coming from Edmonton. From Calgary. And Winnipeg. Lots of flights came from Vancouver, but I didn't see you. So many people! People crying and laughing and kissing and hugging the family waiting for them there. So many people was at the airport yesterday!"

"Why did you go? Didn't I tell you to stop going to the air-port?"

This behaviour developed after the divorce. A voice would notify her of my impending arrival, and she'd show up at Pearson International. Morning, noon and midnight. Airport officials occasionally telephoned Aunt Sofia who would explain

they needed to send my mother home in a taxi. I wasn't scheduled to land, no reunion possible except the one she fancied in
her broken brain.

"I wanted see you."

Perhaps Mrs. Perkins should have joined us. A buffer. I
used to be the cushion—not the best bumper, more like a pin-
cushion—between my folks, but I'd lost the ability to soften any
blows. "I'm not going to tell you when I'm at the airport ever.
Understand? Never. You always want to make a spectacle of
yourself. The grieving Italian mother. I will never allow you to
do that to me again. I'm here now, and this is better than you
deserve."

"If someone told me I'd give birth to a daughter with the
tongue of a serpent—"

"Sure. Because you'd never stoop to puzzle out if I inherited
your venomous nature. You poor victim, oh boo-hoo, no one's
had it harder than you." I wrung my hands for extra theatrics.
They vibrated with rage. "It's too late, Ma. Stop sending me
things. Stop looking for me at the airport. Stop calling the police. Stop looking for me in the bushes around your building.
Stop searching for me or Dad at your ex-sisters-in-law's houses.
Stop. Give it a rest. Please, for the love of God, let us rest."

"Why I should stop looking for you? I don't have anyone
else. What am I supposed to do?" Fat tears rolled down her
cheeks. She grabbed a tissue and rubbed it across her eyes. Her
movements jerky, a probable side effect from forty years—off
and on—of hard-core antipsychotics.

Defeated, I stared at the crocheted tablecloth under the
clear plastic cover.

She huffed and wailed with her mouth open. My mother
looked like a child when she cried. Her face scrunched up, and

she covered her eyes with the backs of her hands to hide that she was weeping. For the millionth time, I wondered about her childhood, about what happened to her, about what it must have been like to grow up in postwar Italy in a family of farmers, born to violent, repressed and oppressive parents, people who were fit to raise livestock, not children.

"Okay, Ma, okay." I apologized and said the coffee was good while it carried an acrid aftertaste that coated my tongue.

"Eat the ricotta torta. I made last night."

The pie tasted off, infused with the scent of mothballs. Sure enough, she'd baked the confection and stored it with chemical pesticides. Later, I'd watch her spray lemon-scented Pledge into the air like room freshener because the perfume worked as protection in her apartment. The skin on her hands was scaly; alabaster cracks peeled with pooled dried blood from using harsh cleaning products without gloves. She washed her dishes with Comet to avoid contamination from germs.

The previous day, she had left the airport alone and called the police to report my assault, believing she heard me screaming, "Mamma, help me. Mamma, there's killer at my door. Mamma, I need you." Then she bought eggs and stayed up late to make my favourite dessert.

I swallowed the coffee and asked for another piece of the pie. "Don't scrimp, Ma. Make it a big one."

Her fridge was almost empty and her cupboards bare. When I questioned her weekly allowance, she showed me a nickel and said, "This what I have lefting. Tomorrow I go bank."

I insisted that we go grocery shopping, but she argued.

"No need." She yanked open the fridge. Inside was a bag of milk, defrosting from the freezer in a plastic jug, a tiny jar with three bulbs of garlic, a small container of store-bought pasta sauce and a watermelon. The wide-open spaces starkly white and cavernous.

I dropped the subject. Better to throw my mental reserves into dragging her to a medical appointment. I took in the view from the balcony. "Centre Island. This is a nice apartment, Ma."

"You like, you come live with me."

She sensed I wasn't being honest. Her questions and non-stop chatter took on a machine-gun barrage. "You see your father all the time, or are you here for a visit him? Where do you work now? What do you do? They don't have that job here in Ontario? Why don't you tell your boss your Mamma needs you? It's no good, me here, you there, your Papa someplace else. We all pay rent. The money will finish. The money will run out. We need a house. We need the home."

I redirected the discussion to the weather, my cat, anything but my father and his sisters. Talking with my mother is like the kindergarten game Telephone. Only there is no class of sticky-sweet preschoolers between us. From my lips to her ears, the firing of synapses, the misunderstandings, the reaction time, the engagement of the nervous system when a comment is perceived as an insult or a slur: It's simply the two of us, always misinterpreted and perplexed. I learned this the hard way: Words—the source of endless wonder for a writer—are worthless in the punishing world of psychosis. Definitions became nonsensical. Sentences and paragraphs of word salad tumbled out of my mother—void of meaning. What I said and what she heard never matched—on one level, this itself is not so dissimilar from regular encounters. Misunderstandings between strangers and friends occurred all the time, complications caused by different interpretations—but there was a conversational thread, a trail of bread crumbs for everyone to find their way. This was never possible with my mother. We didn't even speak the same language to each other. My mother spoke fragmented English, peasant dialect and psychosis-fuelled speech; I spoke patchy dialect mixed with basic English, and rage-full rhetoric when we argued. Confusion reigned supreme.

"If I stay in this apartment one year more, Julian Fantino is going to give me a house. He did it for another two ladies that lived in this building. They left last month. One neighbour said they died, but I know the truth. This place is too small. I move here, I move there, I move around, but there's no room. No backyard. My friend said I should write Fantino because he helped her. He's chief of the Toronto police, and he's Italian. He'll fix this situation for me. He can arrange for me to have a house. Let's write the letter together. You can help me."

"Can I lie down for a bit, Ma?"

She jumped into mothering mode, commenting on how tired I must be from the time difference. I didn't correct her. She'd wake me in an hour.

It made her happy, having me in the other room.

I stretched out on her double bed and felt a serrated blade under my pillow. A bread knife stashed under my head.

"What's this, Ma?"

"Protection. From all the killers in the building."

"What are you going to do? Make them toast? I'm not sleeping here tonight if you don't put the knife back in the kitchen drawer."

"But what if someone comes in?"

"Your door has a lock and a bolt. If we have a problem, we

can call the police." Could someone have 911 on speed dial, I wondered? If anyone did, it was my mom.

Anosognosia, one of schizophrenia's most pervasive and frustrating symptoms, is lack of insight that one is ill. Anosognosia is not denial, not a "difficult client," not plain stubbornness. To fully appreciate the horror of this signpost, I need solely recall the last time I caught a cold or flu and envision the congestion, aches and fever as a permanent state. Did I remember to ingest the prescribed antibiotics consistently? Doubtful. A Temporal Lobe Influenza: the disease that took possession of my mother. Impaired awareness of illness also occurs with Alzheimer's and in individuals who sustained brain injuries.

Because she took her meds randomly, my mother was agitated, and more likely to call the police, make her way to emergency, or harass one of my elderly aunts. On medication, she was a fraction less manic. Age had deflated her rage: She could still hit that opera-level atomic high note but did so less often. The dates on the three blister packs of pills my mother had were for April; it was August.

That afternoon, as we sat in her doctor's office, I watched my mom speak to the people she knew, observed as they took her in with carefully blank expressions. In her interaction with the receptionist, she was blunt; she didn't waste time with pleasantries. Mom jabbered at the young woman while she held the phone receiver to her ear, instructing a caller.

"This my daughter. I come for my needle." My mother headed for a chair.

The receptionist nodded and covered the receiver, "Please have a seat, Lucia."

Every spot in the waiting room filled up as we waited. A television in the far corner played the World Cup: Italy had been knocked out of the competition early on.

It was midafternoon. My mother fell asleep, her head down, tucked in. I did a sidelong scan. She was immensely vulnerable, slumbering in public. I turned away and blinked my eyes at the sports on screen.

My inner critic snapped to attention: look. You look. You don't get the option to turn away now, when she's sitting right next to you. You abandoned her. She barely functions in this big city, this massive country. You speak the language, you navigate everything so much easier, and she struggles every single day. You bear witness. The least a dutiful daughter could do. Look.

I shifted in my seat to face her. At sixty-one, she seemed decades older. Her pudgy features ravaged by an illness that also caused poor self-care habits. She was missing all her top front teeth. Without the protective barrier, her upper lip collapsed in on her mouth. Her skin was wrinkled with deep grooves, fissures lined her cheeks. She'd been a stunning beauty as a young woman. My parents, with their chiselled chins, high cheekbones and flawless skin, made a striking couple.

I sat up straight, and my adjustment woke my mother. She looked up at me and smiled.

The nurse ushered us into a small room. My mother handed over a tiny bottle of liquid meant for the syringe, a small vial filled with clear liquid. The medication she picked up at the pharmacy downstairs.

"Lucy, what happened? We haven't seen you in a while," asked the nurse, her voice warm and welcoming. I almost burst into tears over this simple act of kindness.

"Are you her daughter? You live in Vancouver."

"Yes, I'm visiting." I meant to smile, but it came out more of a grimace, my lips flattening against my teeth, a reflex to stop from welling up.

"You must be very happy, Lucy. I can see it from the smile on your face."

"She the only one I have. And she live too far from me."

I bit my upper lip.

My mother lifted up her skirt. Even in warm weather, she would not give up full-support pantyhose. She pulled down the hosiery on her right side for the needle. The medicine meant to prevent psychotic episodes had to be injected into her thigh. The nurse asked my mother if she remembered which leg she'd been poked in before, so she could alternate, as my mother always felt tender afterwards.

I fidgeted: I crossed my arms. I unfolded them to hang on to my mother's purse for her. Scratching my forehead and my earlobe, I searched the exam room for a focus while shifting my weight. I felt fourteen again: powerless to prevent her pain, unable to break the family curse.

On the way back to her apartment, my mother was subdued. The morning storm clouds had blown out of sight. We stood on the crowded bus, facing west, the sunlight blinding bright.

For dinner, she scorched an onion in reused oil until it blackened and poured store-bought sauce into the pan. The macaroni cooked in an uncovered roasting pan placed on an element.

"Is that safe?"

"They say cooks fast this way. They say no hurt my teeth if cook like this. They say healthier to make in this."

They: the background chatter—the ceaseless din.

After doing the dishes with the soap I'd purchased over her

protests, we agreed on an activity: taking an inventory of all the apparel she owned, clothes she refused to hang in the closet. She produced an enormous haul of blouses and camisoles, neatly folded and proudly shown off. See-through shirts, tank tops with sequins, nylon peignoirs, lacy panties, cotton underwear and flashy polyester numbers in tropical garden prints. She'd stockpiled towels, bed linens, negligées and kitchen utensils into three giant suitcases.

"I bought this one for you because you fat now. XXXL. Three X and one L, maybe it fits you. Who else could take it? I buy for you." She handed me a hideous canary yellow and factory grey T-shirt with silver script that spelled out "Gymnastic Golfing."

"I don't want this. Please spend your money on food."

Her eyes narrowed.

I'd stepped on another mine.

"Who's the Mamma here? I am. Who do you think you are? Lying to me, arriving for one day and forcing me to go to the doctor. You think you know everything? You know nothing. I raised a stupid, selfish daughter."

I sighed. "Okay, Ma. Takes one to know one." I accepted the plain black cotton underwear she'd set aside. "The rest of this cheap crap is no bargain. Please don't wear it when you cook."

The effort required to be together meant when we climbed into bed, we both dozed off fast.

In the morning, while I gathered my backpack and my purse, she whimpered, "Why? Why you have to going? There nothing for you here? Nobody?"

"Please, Ma, please don't—" I begged her not to come downstairs with me, but she insisted on walking me to the bus stop.

)

"When I will see you again? I waited so long, and this is all you give me, one day."

The time between goodbye for now and hello again was never long enough for me; for my mother it seemed an eternity.

The leaves on the maple trees were brilliant hues of emerald. In a few weeks, come October, I'd revel in the season I'd missed the most out west when the greenery switched to ruby, crimson and blood—the colour of family.

"Soon."

The bus turns onto her side street.

"Okay, Ma, give me a hug and go back inside."

She kissed me five times, crying.

"It's okay, Mom. I'm okay, promise. Don't worry about me."

"Who else I can worry for? You're all I have." She walked partway back to the entrance of her building, then stopped to watch me board the bus.

I waved.

She waved back, the way one might to an infant, hand steady as a salute and moving her fingers as if she was patting air. She stood alone against the backdrop of the tall building, a tiny senior, such a contrast from the Titan of my nightmares; a woman abandoned by her parents, lost in the destructive shuffle of a serious brain disorder, missing her only child. We continued to wave to each other as the bus pulled away from the curb. Farewell and welcome look the same, for an instant, were it not for me putting distance between the two of us.

The Sun

(XIX)

She persists and finds aid.

Some mornings, I chanted om—the sound of the planet's vibration—and pretended that the trucks roaring by, the streetcar swishes and honking horns were all humming along to the same rhythm. And nights I sang a mantra or spoke a simple prayer: please help me. Most mornings I woke with good intentions, and then slowly the day fell apart. Ideas, plans, schedules.

At night when I couldn't turn off the worried thoughts, when they rushed around like a truck rumbling down the highway, driven recklessly, no brake pedal, I listened to video astrologers on YouTube to override the anxiety. I played them to quash the panic spirals and cross-referenced their readings. Stormy weather in the week ahead because Mars in Scorpio, part of my chart, was conjunct with my Jupiter sign, Libra. The influence of Mercury retrograde—unresolved issues resurfacing and no signing any contracts. I should be wary about negotiating any-

thing when Venus is at a hard angle to my Sun sign, Aquarius.
Saturn could indicate smooth sailing and attention from VIPS but
also attention from the police.

These horoscopes boiled down to: This could be a rough
week with some lovely moments.

I ordered a chart from the astrologer with the most soothing
voice. I read through the vague descriptors and thought: I paid
money for this. The sentence that confirmed I'd wasted money:
As a small child you may have felt warm and protected in your
family environment.

At our daily check in, after I listed off everything that I suspected was wrong with me, my dad advised, "It's not good you feel
like this. You should go see somebody."

At a walk-in clinic, I cried so hard Dr. Kim could barely
make out what I was saying. She waited patiently for me to
catch my breath between sobs.

"You're not seeing me at my best."

She nodded and offered me another tissue from the box she
held. "I will. Do you have someone you can talk to?" She looked
at my medical file, at the notes she had made during our session.
Dr. Kim had drawn a simple graph, a barebones family tree.
Mother: severely mentally ill. Father: clinical depression. Me:
episodes of melancholy.

"Friends. Do you mean a professional? No."

"There's a lot here. And a lot going on right now. You may
find it helpful to talk to someone."

I don't tell her about the distorted thinking. I have to work
very hard to stay present. I can put up a good front. It looks
like I'm here, talking in the now, listening, answering questions,
but there's this constant pull from the past. An unexpected un-

dercurrent. Like the time I got hit by a wave and somersault-
ed through the water, frantic because I couldn't swim, so close
to shore that when the wave pulled back, it dragged me along
the sand, my arm and thigh scraped as I tried to grab onto
the ground. Then I stood in three feet of water and sputtered
the ocean I'd inhaled out of my lungs. My friend on the beach
laughed until she saw my face: "You're okay. You're safe now."
If life-as-a-metaphor meant feeling comfortable in moving water and cresting high seas, my limited dog-paddling ability and
ill-equipped dinghy posed a problem.

"Do I need a referral to see someone who specializes in
trauma?"

"Yes. I'll send one in so we can get that started. I could also
prescribe something for you—"

This again.

"Do you remember what you were on before?"

"An SSRI that didn't work very well. And then one meant to
help me sleep. I took it every night for two months, and the pill
left a metallic taste in my mouth every morning."

"Let's start small then. We'll try this, and you make an appointment up front to come back and tell me how it's going in a
month. That should give the medication time to adjust to your
system. But if you have any uncomfortable side effects, come
back sooner and we'll make an adjustment. And we'll get you in
to see someone too."

Later, I went through my journals and couldn't find a record of the second medication. I found new moon charts, and
vision boards. Notebooks full of ideas and no follow through. I
clambered into bed. At two in the afternoon, I couldn't keep my
eyes open.

On a mild autumn day, I set out for an appointment with Dr. Andreev, the psychiatrist at the mental health centre. On the subway ride to the building on College Street, a feeling of déjà despair wafted through me. Apprehension about the meeting. The last time I met with a psychiatrist, it was my father's—a fifteen-minute session for the doctor to check my dad's meds and ask how life was treating him. I asked questions and persisted through the condescending tone. That guy had no interest in what I'd learned about mental illness in my role as amateur detective and armchair psychologist over a lifetime of trying to pin down the family plague.

Dr. Andreev welcomed me into a spacious office. His windows looked out into downtown on a sunny and mild Toronto day. I wished I were riding a bike on Centre Island.

"The report from your doctor says there's been trauma but not many details."

I nodded and focused on my hands in my lap. When I opened my mouth, no words came out. I shook my head and shrugged one shoulder. "My mom was ill. And violent. It took a toll. It's still taking a toll."

Dr. Andreev signaled to the box of tissues near me.

"When do you remember the abuse starting?"

"It was always part of our everyday life."

"Were Child Services called in?"

I gathered he was taking measurements. "Yes. Once when I was almost twelve. But my dad promised the social worker the problem would be solved in Italy."

He waited for me to stop blowing my nose.

"Do you have any issues with drugs or alcohol?"

"Coffee. And sugar. And too much salt."

"Do you experience any euphoria translated into dangerous

behaviour? Harmful behaviours?" He offered a list and nothing twigged.

"Maybe reckless spending? But that's if I stay up too late and get on Amazon. Then I buy a lot of books. I've got a lot of unread books."

"Do you go into debt over these purchases?"

"Everything racks up debt when you don't have a steady job. Bills are due that I can't pay. I've worked since I was sixteen, and the last time I didn't have a guaranteed gig, I didn't function very well. I prefer to keep busy."

Then I bring up the topic I've been wondering about. Possible misdiagnosis. How what looked like depression could have been something else that I'd never heard of until recently. "I've been reading about the research done by a professor of clinical psychology at Harvard on something called C-PTSD."

"The C stands for?"

"Complex." Never bring your own research to a psych fight. "No. That's not in the DSM."

"I know. But it might be one day." Tears streamed down my face. I was dabbing my cheeks as much as I could. But this wasn't my first time at the evaluation rodeo, and I wouldn't let someone from a profession that had repeatedly let my family down talk over me. "Until the DSM was updated in the late 1980s, LGTBQ people were being treated as ill, and some were even treated with aversion therapy. I read a memoir of a woman who was given electroshock treatments because she was a lesbian."

"Do you have nightmares about the abuse?"

"No—"

"Then it's not PTSD."

I can't explain about the evil presence I sometimes dream

about, that I sometimes wake up with, certain it's in my room. I don't even know the dark mirages are symptomatic of night tremors, an issue that affects children and adults.

Dr. Andreev asked about my medication history. He suggested my dosage had never been high enough to cause any lasting positive change. "That's an issue when family doctors prescribe antidepressants." He noted that most people have to stay on them for the rest of their lives, and the worst side effects (numbness, exhaustion) don't go away, so it would be a matter of finding drugs that didn't cause those additional problems when possible.

"I don't think you understand. You're not seeing me at my best. I need to get my life—"

"Yes?"

I wasn't in a reactive relationship any more, and I'd avoided ugly boundary entanglements as much as possible as an adult. The rare case flew under my radar, particularly when my detection system went offline, usually because I felt vulnerable. Like right then.

I didn't know up from down, only anxiety, only a desperate need to feel like I could manage again, in a life mostly together instead of frayed at the seams and falling apart. I was hard-pressed to think of anything I did to look after myself. For years, at every medical checkup, when a doctor would press a stethoscope against my back and say "Take a deep breath," they would have to say, "Again, and a little deeper please." You could forget how to breathe naturally, normally when you have been ill. You might forget there was ever a time when you felt safe enough to take a deep breath. You might not know until years had passed that what every doctor noticed and you didn't was that your shallow breathing meant you'd been afraid and holding your breath for a very long time.

I didn't say: Pull out the tarot, try to predict the future.

He wrote the name of a medication on the back of his business card. Told me to get the book *Mind over Mood* out of the library and to start cognitive behavioural therapy.

I took his card and thanked him. Out on College Street, in the middle of the afternoon, the city filled with people on their way to or from coffee break, to or from heartbreaks, to or from work. I looked back at the building and knew I would never call to book a follow-up.

My muscles ached and joints stiffened with soreness. I felt arthritic in my neck and shoulders. My throat was itchy and tender, perhaps with the strep throat I used to get all the time. I retreated into spending time alone.

I had no desire to see anyone or to be seen. A heavy constriction in my lungs felt like all the air was being compressed, slowly, out of my chest: I breathed slowly to steady my thoughts. I felt like a diver being lowered into the depths of the sea in a shark-proof cage, realizing at the last moment that I was not properly equipped. The wetsuit, another layer of skin, wasn't enough. I needed gills. I needed to breathe under water.

One morning, I woke up hissing.

I sat straight up in bed, disoriented, not fully aware of my surroundings. My eyes adjusted to the dark as dim light streamed in the window from streetlamps. The digital clock read 3:33 AM on this fourth night in a row I had woken at 3:30, restless, anxious. I focused on my bed, my room. My nightmare had morphed into night terrors. Moments before, in the dream, I had been in another apartment, a high-rise that I believed to be home. Faint light filtered in from the floor-to-ceiling sliding glass door of the balcony. I was uneasy, unable to imagine how I had ended up in this unfamiliar place, furnished like a bland hotel room. Every dream friend was a stranger, an unrecognizable face. They would come in, talk for a bit, and then their faces would twist and contort into severe expressions of grief. People kept coming to visit me, and in the brief time of the visit, they ended up sickly, so overtaken by irrational thoughts that each one jumped off the balcony.

Each time, I yelled, "Wait! Stop!"

A voice whispered, "There's a malevolent presence here." I spun around and couldn't find the source.

Not possible, I thought, I would know. Full of false bravado.

I heard a bizarre mix of speech and sound, not one voice but many, murmuring conversations, unkind laughter. A swirling sensation came over me as I spun around, looking for the source of the shadow presence I finally sensed. I looked around the room. This couldn't be how I lived, where I lived. Where was my furniture? My bookshelves? The buzzing sound of talk grew louder.

The cautionary voice spoke again. "Protect yourself. Dangerous. Unsafe."

More mumbling drowned out the guardian voice.

"What do I do? Who is it?" I felt something, someone walk past me. I heard laughter. A cackle. My mother's laugh.

I hissed like a feral cat. I turned 360 degrees, standing on the same spot, sibilating to every corner of the room, furious with myself for not being aware, sooner, that trouble was brewing. No retreat, stand firm, I thought, it's dangerous to be this oblivious. First I felt fear, then fury.

Spittle lined my lips as I kept hissing in my sleep, defending my space. I wanted to ferret out the evil, to retaliate and destroy the demon that deprived me of a mom. "You can't catch me. You can't hurt me."

I woke up cold, hissing and shivering. I kicked the sheets off myself as my eyes adjusted. What if a menace had followed me back from the world of dreams? My breathing quieted. As in the nightmare, I sensed nothing. The hissing woke me, I realized; I wiped my mouth.

Was I the gatekeeper between two realms I couldn't identify? "You will not get past me," I said aloud, in case. And then I hissed.

For the rest of the day, I felt the chill of tiredness and terror.

When I told my father about the dream, he had no doubt about its significance. My mother, born to the malevolent stregas, was trying to get at me again.

The following summer in Toronto is a season of amplified sound. Wires buzz, car horns blare, people yell obscenities at slow drivers. The air conditioned to a hum. Every voice is louder in hot weather, not muffled by snow or slush.

A cool August meant sleep was possible. Rest from unrelenting heat. Even with this weather bonus, I called my dad and broke down over the phone. Pounding the employment pavement meant mounting humiliation.

"Think how hard it was for the people who came here and didn't understand anything, No English. Maybe they couldn't read or write even in their first language. That's not you."

He assumed agreement in my silence.

"Look at the news. See the people in Syria—they have hardship and real suffering. People lose their life because a crazy stupid man is in charge. People try to cross the sea in the boat and wish they live in a place like Canada. Is not your situation."

"I've made a mess of this life, and I don't know how to fix it. I can't get out of bed. I'm struggling to get dressed, get up, get to another job agency."

"Please, you know how upsets me to see you like this. What I can do?"

"Nothing."

"You should go look in the mirror," he says, repeating his familiar advice. "You no cheats nobody. You no steal from the people. You no kill nobody."

I agree to go over the next day for lunch.

At Islington station, waiting for the south-travelling bus, my brain feels stuffed with cotton. It may not be good to visit the geography of my nightmares. Whenever I dream I am stuck, not moving forward, that I never left, it is in this suburb of concrete and cars.

I sat at dad's small table while he cooked bucatini noodles with tomato sauce. He'd initially suggested going out, but I wasn't in the mood. After the mishap at No Frills, I didn't want to expose myself to any more run-ins with my mother, who still roamed the neighbourhood, searching for my dad, pestering my aunt enough to warrant a restraining order.

I asked after my aunts.

"Your mother showed up at your Aunt Sofia's house again last night. Middle of the night, banging on the door. Asking you to come home and stop working as a prostitute. Then she asked Sofia to make friendship. Can you believe? She has no shame. No feeling."

"What do you mean, she was in the neighbourhood? Why didn't you tell me?"

"I didn't want to upset you."

I stopped eating. "I can't believe you. I can't believe how

many times we have the same conversation over and over and nothing changes. I need the warning. I ask you to give me the information I need to keep myself safe, and you can't even do that. You don't—

"I don't want you to get upset. You see how you're getting upset. That woman ruined everything for us. I don't want—"

"I'm upset with you, not Mom. I'm upset with me. I keep trusting you, and there's no reason to trust you. You've never given me a reason to have faith that anything would be taken care of."

"Me, you don't trust me? I put you before me my whole life whatever you needed, whatever you wanted. You needed books, I buy, you needed clothes, I buy—"

I got up and scraped my dish into the garbage. I filled the sink with soapy water and refused to speak.

"Eufemia, please. I can't stand to see you like this."

"So look away. Did I ask you to look? Who's asking you to look? You avoided looking, avoided dealing with the problem the whole time the awful situation was right in front of you. Why pay attention now? Why do the one thing I ask of you?"

"Here we go. I do everything for everybody, and I'm the bad guy. Better I should die now. No one appreciates sacrifice. It's a waste."

"Why can't you understand why it's important for me to know so I can keep myself safe? Since you couldn't do it twenty years ago, try now and I'll make a decision like 'today's a day I stay home' instead of coming here not knowing and then running into her." I cursed myself for forgetting my sunglasses and my hooded jacket. Not that the clothes made for a perfect disguise, but I felt less exposed, less anxious when I covered up, even though I probably drew more attention to myself. Like a pathetic spy-school dropout.

I washed the dishes while my dad continued to mutter about how no one understood the efforts he'd gone to and everyone was selfish and self-absorbed.

Shouting at a senior who loves me. I knew it was ridiculous, but I couldn't unhook the rage. Like burs stuck all over me.

I shouted, "I'm going home," and refused the offer of a lift to the subway. The anger had a grip that wouldn't let go, and I didn't want to say thank-you for anything. I wanted to vent resentment.

At my apartment, I got back into bed and turned off my phone. I tried to will my body into calm, but I couldn't shake off the tremors. My hands shook. I yanked the duvet over my head and slept for four hours. When I woke, I lit a candle and placed it in front of my parents' wedding photo. Then I called my dad to apologize.

"I don't know what's wrong with me."

"I thought you were finished. Thought I broke you. Too much stress is not good for living."

"Can I go see Victor?"

Victor, my father's parapsychologist-tarot-reading- feng-shui-master, was gregarious and easy to talk with for a guy dabbling in the woo-woo world.

After my dad's psychotic break, when he spoke of my mother's witchcraft, Victor had sat patiently with him and prescribed a homeopathic treatment—a Bach flower remedy. He'd told me I needed to form a mudra with my hand when I felt stressed, to stop the energy from dissipating and running out of me. The second time I'd tagged along on a checkup of my dad's, Victor interrupted himself to give me a warning. "You should protect the space where you sleep better. Throw white light around it as you're falling asleep."

"How?"

"How? With your mind, what else?" He looked at my father—a look that said they don't teach this stuff in school and they really should.

Books on feng shui flourished in his waiting room as well as annual prospects for each sign of the Chinese zodiac. I looked up my sign to see how the Rooster would fare. Then I perused my father's (Tiger) and my mother's (Rat). Animals that would never hang out together. In the mythology of the birth of this astrology, Buddha hosted a race and invited all the animals in the kingdom. Twelve showed up, and the rotation of their honorary years is based on the order of making it through the finish line. The Rat cheated by hitching a ride on the Ox, and that's how it arrived before every other critter. Under the Rat, in the weaknesses category: unstable.

Victor called my name and led me into his office space. He listened as I poured out the confusing parts of my panic spiral. I couldn't figure out what to do or how I would do it. Look after my dad. Manage the unknowable future. I'd kept myself so busy before; now, without work, my days had no structure and no meaning.

"When he called, your dad told me he was worried about you. Your energy is like his was when he first came to see me. Maybe not as bad but very low." He pulled a folder from his desk drawer and labelled it with my name, birthdate and time of birth. Then, on a blank unlined sheet he drew the outline of a body. He traced the outer lines with three circles.

"This is your aura in the world. Right now it's dark grey and full of holes, an energy leak from all the psychic attacks. The second layer is dull as stone too. When the outer layer gets hit repeatedly, the second is weakened. If the first layer, the one that's like another skin, is also depleted, then that's crisis time. That's health issues. Insomnia, no focus, no strength."

"I think I've always been tired."

"You don't have to believe what I'm saying to you. It doesn't matter. I'm telling you what's happened to you—who knows how many lifetimes. This could be old pain."

"I don't remember a time when I didn't feel exhausted."

Victor held up a hand to stop me while he made notes on my chart. "First the cord between you and your mother has to be cut. She's not well. It's not her fault. Not completely. You have a choice to make."

"You mean not being in contact."

"It's up to you. If you can do it and stay strong, but the umbilical energy cord between you two has to be cut. She's not a problem you can fix. You come into the world unprotected. And the people around you have to protect you."

I told him I had malocchio removal when I was a baby, when I was six months old.

"You and everybody else who was born to Southern Italian parents. That's why they don't pay compliments to the baby."

"I guess that's how people coped with high infant mortality rates, and with living in horrendous poverty when no one had access to education."

"Listen, not everything everyone thought was backwards then. They understood essentials no one thinks about now. You spend time around someone like your mother, and you will get sick too. Look at your father. Look at the difference in him now to ten years ago. He was almost dead."

"That's because he wouldn't make a decision to get out sooner."

Victor believes what my dad believes—which is based on

what Victor said—so this weird spooky-spirit-sickened-séance stuff comes full circle. All roads lead to hexes.

I left his office with a candle and instructions to let it burn for three days straight. At night, or if I needed to leave my apartment, I had to place the candle in my bathtub with nothing flammable nearby. The candle sat on a white plate that Victor had cleansed and given back to me.

"Whichever way the wax goes, put everything after the three days in a plastic bag and bring the bag to me. Leave it with Isabelle at the front desk."

Two weeks later I returned for the analysis.

"At least you didn't wait as long as your father to come for help." He gives me another white candle. One to light every morning at the same time and speak directly to God. "Or Spirit, or universe, whatever you prefer. Every morning, after you light this, you tell the universe everything you are grateful for. Say thank-you and really mean it; say it with your heart full of love. You need to start when the next new moon finishes." He checked his calendar. "And go for twenty days, up to the full moon. Please make sure the space around your bed is clean and clear. We need for that space to be protected. You like to write, so write down what happens in your dreams. Pay attention to what happens. Make an appointment to come see me again in a month."

At the next visit, Victor looked me over and wrote more notes. He prepared a package for me—the contents of which contained the melted candle and other materials.

"Leave this behind your bed for three nights. Put it in one

spot and don't touch it. On the fourth day, you need to throw it into water. Running water is better than the lake, but you can go to the beach. You have to turn your back to the water, and throw it behind you. Make sure you set yourself up. You have to throw it hard so it lands in the water. You can be near the edge. Then you walk away. Don't turn back to look at the package. You can't, you understand? Walk away. Go home. If this is a place you go to all the time, don't go for a while. A week."

"What if it's a body of water I pass every day on transit?"

He thought about it. "That should be okay."

Days later, I waited for a lone moment on a pedestrian bridge over the Don River. I didn't want to have to explain to anyone walking past, "I'm using the river to perform a curse removal. I know it sounds like a metaphor, but listen, can you scoot away? I have to sidestep an Orpheus manoeuvre now, and if you distract me, I might turn the wrong way and be faced with demons forever." I calculated the angle to make sure I didn't throw the package on the banks. Then I hurled it. I walked away, not looking back.

Overhead the sun shone. A breeze blew down to the lake. I heard the traffic of the parkways and walked home, stopping at my favourite café to grab a coffee.

Later that night, I told my dad everything had gone smoothly, nothing felt different.

"That's the mistake I made." My dad had done this treatment in the early days of seeing Victor. "I threw this little bottle into Lake Ontario, and then I turned around to look at it. In that moment, everything came back to me. All my bad luck, my bad life with your mother. Every humiliation she put me through. But you didn't look, and that's good."

I knew this story. Back when I first heard it, months after

that visit in my early twenties where I'd refereed my parents' wrestling match for hours, I'd thought my father was gone. Or that the person I thought was my father had never really existed except as a figment I'd created. That the real man was so flawed and superstitious, he'd believe a bottle could contain evil spirits and unleash sickness.

"I guess I learned from your mistake."

"That's life. Make a mistake, learn, make a mistake, learn. You try not to be make the same mistakes."

Judgement
(XX)

*She makes peace with the
messengers of responsibility.*

In my old apartment in Vancouver, before I moved back to Toronto, I answered a knock early one Sunday evening and found a police officer standing outside my door. My roommate, Ruth, was out. I assumed something must have happened in the neighbourhood and that the officer was going door to door in the co-op, to warn everyone. Ridiculously handsome, tall and broad-shouldered, he looked as if he'd walked out of a GQ magazine cover shoot, or maybe worked as a stripper in a cop uniform until he landed his big acting break.

I wore baggy lime track pants and a turquoise sweatshirt, my doing-laundry attire. I had my hair piled in a messy topknot, held in place with a scrunchie.

He said, "Don't be alarmed." Even his voice was gorgeous; soothing, like dark hot chocolate swirled with organic peppermint. "Is your name Eufemia?"

" — I'm a little alarmed that you know my name."

"Your mother called the police in Toronto and reported you as a missing person."

"Oh. Would you like to come in?"

"Sure. Your neighbours don't need to hear this."

I closed the door behind the officer as he stepped into our kitchen. With his back turned to me, I reached up to undo my bun. I realized in time it would look mildly lascivious and that nothing would make my comfortable, kaleidoscope-coloured outfit appear adult-in-control.

I fiddled with my silver acorn pendant. "My mother is severely mentally ill. I've been told she has a file with the police in Toronto the size of a telephone book."

"Right, well, they gave us a call. Someone sent you an email, but you didn't reply. We have to investigate every claim."

"Oh. I didn't realize. I'm not missing. I've cut off contact with my mother because I find it difficult to deal with her."

In a misguided attempt to keep in touch, I had given my cell phone number to my mother, thinking I would limit the aggravation for my roommate and everyone in my dad's family if she could reach me. In the first week, she left seventeen messages, shouting, screaming, badgering and bullying threats that went on for five minutes at a time. I called her, told her I couldn't take it anymore and that I would be changing my number.

"You're sick," she said. "You need Mamma to look after you."

I said I was sorry, I couldn't listen to her anymore, and hung up.

I explained it all to the officer as he nodded.

"Does your mother speak English?"

"Yes. She understands too, until someone like you shows up and then she'll fake that she doesn't speak the language, doesn't know what you're saying."

The officer looked sympathetic. "At least this was quick. Sometimes we go to ten houses before we find who we're looking for. It only took us an hour to find you."

I resisted the urge to say, "Because I wasn't missing." Tomorrow could find me holed up in a Chevron gas station washroom, cutting off all my hair and dying it blond. Let's see how fast you find me then, Officer Hottie. You had a sweet deal here, an easy patrol, a non-suspect to apprehend and a short report to file. Next time, I'll pull a full fugitive.

More cops will track me down — first thing in the morning, middle of the day, late in the evening and once nearing midnight — and ask me to call my mother, as if regular conversation and contact with her delinquent daughter could stop her psychosis from taxing their overstressed system.

Sometimes I'll interrogate them, "Are you saying she presented as coherent and sane? Isn't there a computer file with my mother's name in it? Doesn't it note what transpired in our past and that I live in hiding from her? What makes you think she'll listen to me this time?" Often, I apologize.

I ordered the police file on my family. Filled out the forms, got my dad's signature, paid for the archived transcript. I hoped for a bulleted list of every visit with details. I received a sheet of paper with six dates and no other particulars — due to concerns for her privacy. Over twenty-five law enforcement visits, proof of the burdensome past, weren't included on the document. I wasn't granted access to a thorough account. The printout was an incomplete list of interventions that jostled my father's memories:

- The time two officers came to investigate the hit-and-run and recommended professional help for my mother that led to her diagnosis.
- The time an officer showed up with the business card of an Italian social worker and advised my dad to get out. He'd skimmed the file before answering the call and said, "Sir, you can't continue to live like this."
- The time my father apologized profusely to an officer for my mother's obscenity-strewn tirade. He'd served notice that Mom was in violation of the law, missing her court date for shoplifting. The man replied, "You're saying sorry to me? Buddy, I feel sorry for you."
- The time a squad car stopped by with an officer answering the call Mom made about an attempted burglary to find the basement windows had been smashed from the inside. The guilty hammer lay nearby, in plain view, on the china cabinet.
- The time my mother assaulted a nurse at Dad's work (butchery requires a full-time medic on hand). The nurse offered to press charges to help her friend, my father. The officers went to the house and delivered a stern lecture, refusing biscotti and espresso.
- The time four officers came and my mother fed them wine and prosciutto while my father burned with humiliation. She told them her husband refused to sleep with her, and invited them to return for dinner anytime. In parting, one said, "Sure. Next time you can make us spaghetti," and everyone except my father laughed.

It's simple: in a fair and kind society, police wouldn't be tasked with the role of front-line mental health workers. We wouldn't close our hearts to the suffering of others. We wouldn't blame people for their illnesses. We wouldn't criticize. We wouldn't invest in comparison. We wouldn't pretend that a one-size-fits-all remedy exists for the pain that pulses through the heart of another. We would pause before offering advice—remain silent, attentive and humane. Imagine a future where no one would feel shunned when they experienced the onset of schizophrenia or another serious brain disorder. No secrets and no shame. No person disrespected or disregarded; no one would ever feel ashamed, isolated, humiliated, insignificant, belittled or better-off dead—because they would be treated with dignity. Our differences, our fear, would shrivel up, while our connections, our compassion would be boundless—expanding out further and further— magnified to match the size of our universe.

Mercy never expires.

Empathy never ends.

THE WORLD.

The World
(XXI)

*The querent reaches a stage of
completion.*

After our goodbye, twelve blocks away from my
mother's apartment in Etobicoke, I skulked
off the bus and walked west. Every ten feet, I
looked behind me. I didn't want her to figure out where my
father lived. The restraining order Aunt Sofia had taken out
against my mother awarded as much safety as pocket lint.

I called my father and asked if he had time to hang out, if
I could see him before I went back to the city. I'd slept poorly
through my mother's snores.

He'd been expecting my call. "You joke? Sure I coming get
you."

I stood on the corner of Lakeshore Boulevard and the street
I grew up on, and recalled what my cousin Jerry recently said
to me: "Your father looks good. He's happy. He's like a new
man, with a new lease on life. He's like the man I remember

he used to be when we were kids. I keep expecting him to say 'everybody in the car, we're going to High Park for ice cream' or something."

It was true. My father's essence, the part of him that seemed like it had ebbed away, permanently eroded by his time with my mother, had returned. He was funny and philosophical again, with a handful of obsessive-compulsive moments when he dwelled on every material thing he'd worked so hard for and lost.

Once again, I misunderstood his directions and found myself in the wrong spot when he pulled up. I dashed across the street before the light changed and jumped in the front passenger seat.

"Tutte okay?" He reached over and pinched my arm gently.

"No. Not really."

"Better forget about."

"Papa, please."

"I know, I know, easy to say, not easy to do. But what you can do?"

He made us spaghetti with meatballs for lunch, my favourite comfort food, using Aunt Sofia's sauce. He quoted his favourite passages from the Bible, talked about how his bad experiences have brought him closer to God. Every morning he recited the rosary. Every day he attended Mass.

"The Bible say, no sense living unhappy life."

"I haven't read that part. It says a bunch of crazy things too."

"No make your life more hard then has to be."

I smacked my forehead. "Now you tell me. Too late."

"Never too late. Every day new day. You wake up, first thing you say, 'Thanks God for new day, please no let me make sin to nobody today,' especially with the stupid people who just here to make problem. And life goes on."

"Yes."

"Remember what I was say to you. You was see her, she was see you. You was do like the good daughter do. You should be live your life now. Forget the passato. Like the English say, when the milk is fall down, no can pick it up no more. What's use to cry?' I know. Easy for me to say."

No sentence my father started with "Like the English say" has ever sounded like the original phrase.

"When I'm no longer part of this world, I want for you to be okay."

"Come on, I was starting to feel better. What is wrong with you?"

I detect the worry in his eyes. The crease in his brow. The "never enough" thought process that is my inheritance. After every meal, I lugged groceries on transit across the city. Staples I could easily purchase at the Loblaw's across the street, but for my dad buying more than he needed and insisting I haul the rest home.

"Put an apron on you, and you'd be the affectionate mother I never had."

"When could we ever have a meal like this before?" he asked. "Just sitting, eating and talking about the news, or the weather, or what's gone on in the world?"

He meant nobody screaming, breaking dishes, or burning food. He thought about my mother still. We both did. Had there been a network of serious assistance, a way of helping her, or a method of true caregiver respite, we might have coped. She might have thrived. The simplest pleasures are the ones most often taken for granted in this life: a quiet lunch shared with cherished souls is high on the list.

An old folk tradition from Bonefro required mourners to set

a meal aside for the dish to be consumed by a stranger as a ritual to honour the deceased. I include an extra plate for Mom, ever hopeful she gains nourishment.

I made one last attempt, three more times, to stay in contact with my mother. What I mean is that the carousel ride continued. I didn't consult the tarot, or survey the opinion of friends or ask my father for his thoughts. I studied the calendar above my desk. I was forty-one and enrolled in a graduate program of creative writing based in Toronto, offered by Guelph University. In between classes and hanging out at my dad's, I met with new friends, drank coffee and discussed books and craft with other writers. An aggressive infection had seized me. My fever spiked, and pain surged through me when I brushed my teeth. Multiple appointments with specialists couldn't determine the cause. The aches dredged up decades-old anguish.

I subtracted my age when I first felt truly terrified of my mother: five. The mathematic result — I counted thirty-six years of dealing with broken heartedness and failed diplomacy. The same length of time my parents' marriage had lasted.

In the quiet balm of my modest apartment, I said out loud, "I've had enough."

For her birthday, Christmas and Easter, I lit candles and followed the advice given by the astrologer in Vancouver — I focused on the flame and prayed, asking my guardian spirit to speak with my mom's and relay a simple message: an apology sent with love.

A grief counsellor suggested engaging in acceptance exercises with the aid of a photograph. Endorsing non-aerobic activity is a hobby of mine, I told her, and chose an image of three-year-old me. The television, a prized indicator of our success, is the centre focus of the picture. I stand off to the side, hair in puny pigtails, crooked bangs, the serious expression of a child who tries to stay out of trouble and fails. I'm wearing a snazzy dress—white top accentuated by a red collar, cuffs, suspenders and pleated skirt. Stitched to the collar is a tie with black-and-white polka dots: toddler fashionista. Prodded by my mother-photographer, I hold the skirt out, ready to curtsy. In two years, I'll meet my beloved gran. In four years, I'll learn to read and write: this permits me to escape the confinement of a suffocating small-world view. In sixteen years, education will be my passport away from a hostile environment. At first (and for a long while), I won't succeed, but I will try, try again. In thirty-eight years, the photo will be pinned to the bulletin board above my writing desk. I glance up at her—she has no idea what lies ahead, but her worried face knows fear. Her heart will shatter, and her skin will bruise. She will probe ways to turn wounds into words: she will chase dreams, they won't chase her.

Things could have been so much worse, according to my dad. I agree with him ninety-nine percent of the time. The other one percent I argue, obstinate and loud, because trauma stories, these epics, live outside time.

The legacies carry on, the plot never lost, only complicated. Hurt is inherited, wounds get passed down. With tarot readings, astrology consultations and the occasional palm read, I'm fending off inevitable chaos. A few will remind me they're not psychic. As if I didn't know. As if I believed the future could be predicted.

I listen for a comforting phrase: everything will be okay. My home is safe. The worst is over. The next phase of life is about enjoyment.

The soothing words act as a balm. I nod. Exhale. Inhale. In the space of a single breath, so much can happen. Shoulders relax, lungs expand, the heartbeat slows—in the period that follows, I can plan. I can fix. I can find my way out of the maze.

Most often I did this through writing.

In workshops, the banter of feedback focuses on pivotal moments. The narrative progresses from inciting incident to rising action through to the climax where the tension peaks, trailed by falling action and resolution. The plot graph includes a series of higher stakes. The protagonist must change or stands to lose dearly. Redemption, revelation and resolved conflicts—stories with tied-up loose ends, some with a bow—were brought to class as offerings to the muses and fellow students.

But whose life mimicked that sequence? When catastrophe strikes, people are flattened. My family remains busted. I don't expect this to transform. At times, I could barely register forward momentum, let alone follow a chronicle arrow up and up and away. Occasionally a story and its human host gets stuck, suspended in a state of survival, fighting stagnation. Memories don't live merely in the mind: recollections weave through DNA, amass in body tissue and accumulate in meridian points.

I wonder: could synapses formed in fear stop lapping a panic track?

Did I create a thicker fog around myself, a pea-souper that misted over reason, in the years I strove to make sense of our saga? Or did I shine a flashlight into dark corners and root out my oldest companions: monsters?

A Pandora's box opened when my parents married, and inside that container was all the help of the cursed Hope Diamond. As the only daughter of an only son, childless, the end of the tale—one that contained the greatest hits of poverty, misery, misogyny, three generations of maternal madness and a few of paternal melancholy, I wonder how the story ends. What lies pressed between the pages of the Book of Destiny printed and bound on the day of my birth?

This much I know: Nothing is written until a scribe is born.

Someone picks up a pen, or gathers her listeners.

Tells a story, or recites a tale.

Builds a bridge from their world to ours: offers connection, gives us a hand so we can climb out of the gutted space we may have been living in, studying the sky. No longer troubling deaf heaven with bootless cries, we might look upon ourselves and bless the sum of all who came before us, woven into the tapestry of this world and tethered together, each of us playing a part in what is to come.

Acknowledgements

For her faith in this project, dedication as a publisher and craft as a poet, I am multiple life-times indebted to Mona Fertig: eternal thanks. Pearl Luke worked tirelessly with generous editorial insight and offered superb guidance to bring this book into the world: mille grazie. Mark Hand, huge thanks for the gorgeous cover and beautiful book design. Judith Brand, many thanks for the skilful copyediting.

Leanne Milech and Mo Riche, wonderful first readers, I am enormously grateful for their hearty feedback and early help: I'm treating for dinner till the end of time. Deepest, I mean Mariana Trench-level, gratitude.

I have been blessed to know many encouraging and inspiring souls: Leonarda Carranza, Terri Favro, Becky Blake, Nancy Jo Cullen, Carmelinda Scian, Maria Meindl, and Kilby Smith-McGregor—also the amazing Ayelet Tsabari, and the phenomenal Kathy Friedman. Susan Scott, I bow to your genius. For the kind assistance offered during earlier incarnations of this story: Rocco Fantetti, Linda Burchill, Barbara Fee, Nicole Chovil, Mary Rose MacLachlan, Derek Capitaine, Micki Maunsell, Sarah Armenia, Elizabeth Oliver, Tanya D'Anger, Delia De Santis and the late Venera Fazio.

Thanks also to the members of the BC Schizophrenia Society, Canadian Mental Health Association Richmond Branch, and Mood Disorders of British Columbia.

Paleolithic versions of this project were read at two different reading series run by Sandra Cardinal (Red Rocket) and Maria Meindl (Draft), and I remain immensely thankful for their warmth, those opportunities and their ongoing community-building.

Brett Reynolds let me insert anecdotes about my father into articles about teaching English as a Second Language and offered his invaluable assessments with much kindness. Claudia Petrescu and Stefan Pasztor, fabulous folks, trained me for the teaching biz and are two of the finest instructors ever. Special thanks to Licia Canton and Domenic Cusmano, gifted people, for all the work they do making space for other artists.

Excerpts from "The High Priestess" were previously published in two separate essays, "Scribo ergo sum" and "Something Is Lost and Can't Be Found," which appeared in *Exploring Voice: Italian Canadian Female Writers*, a special issue of *Italian Canadiana* (Volume 30, 2016), edited by Venera Fazio and Delia De Santis, published by the Frank Iacobucci Centre for Italian Canadian Studies, Department of Italian Studies, University of Toronto.

I count my lucky stars for my Writer's Studio and Guelph friends, instructors and fellow creators with much appreciation for all the inspiration, dedication and guidance offered — especially Betsy Warland, Wayde Compton, Camilla Gibb and Joe Fiorito.

For the generous support of my writing through timely grants of funds or spaces and locations over the years, I'm grateful to the BC Arts Council, the Canada Council for the Arts, Sage Hill Writing and the lovely Laura K. Bird. For the computer tech aid: Matthew Mallon, Cathy and Jason Leslie, Mary and Maury Larino, and Ayelet Tsabari.

The planets aligned to bring members of my Humber College family into orbit: Mark Andrade, Catherine Aherne, Maria-Lucia Di Placito, Miriam Novick, Jennifer Winfield — I benefit tremendously from your hive wisdom and knowing you marvellous peeps: a concrete figure would be incalculable.

Many thanks to the thoughtful spirit Franc Jamieson, for the job that led to meeting Vera Beletzan, an extraordinary human. Thanks also to Prasad Bidaye for all the writerly encouragement. A simple dictionary search for "godsend" would produce a photo of Meaghan Strimas: forever and ever, thank you. The members of the *Humber Literary Review* collective, most especially the multi-talented Dave Miller, make putting an excellent magazine together look effortless while also making the world a better place: infinite thanks.

The Rider-Waite-Smith deck is full of powerful symbols and archetypes. Designed by Pamela Coleman Smith and published in 1910, the cards were considered innovative and intricate; they continue to be popular with readers. I purchased mine in a fluorescent-lit bookstore chain in Sherway Gardens mall when I was a teen; I'd never heard of tarot, or of the superstition that people shouldn't purchase a deck but be gifted one. No child of devout and devoted Roman Catholics would ever receive "an instrument of divination" for a Christmas present. The package is well-worn and held together with masking tape, but I have them still. With me through every move from province to province, from place to place, and from desk to bookshelf, each time I unpacked them, I knew I was home.

My father always says there are two kinds of people in the world—those who help and those who harm. The first goes through life's difficulties, comes out the other side and thinks to themselves: "I don't want anyone to have it as hard as I did. I'll help everyone I can." The second experiences life's dilemmas and thinks to themselves: "If it was a hardship for me, it should be hard for everybody. I'm not lifting a finger to assist anyone." Cathy Sostad, the first of the first, has a heart like none other I've encountered: profound thanks.

A note about the language in *My Father,*
Fortune-tellers & Me

A Romance language that evolved from Vulgar Latin (the vernacular of the people), Neapolitan has over six million speakers and has been influenced by Arabic, French, Greek and Spanish. Molisan, the language spoken by my parents, is considered a Napoletano dialect (named for the Kingdom of Naples, not the city).

Even within the region, subtle variations in speech patterns can occur between neighbouring villages. I learned this when my father's cousin's son said I spoke "like someone from Bonefro," and I was in a township twelve kilometres away from our village. Before the advent of the internet, I referred to my mother tongue as Bonefran. In conversations with my folks, we frequently switched from English to Molisan to a mixture: Italish.

I tried to learn standard Italian at university. For a brief time, I sounded scholarly, but I felt pompous and pretentious, pushing out extended vowels felt like putting on airs. I didn't realize the source of my frustration until later—an essential part of myself was splintering off when my mind began erasing words from the spoken language in favour of the written one: I couldn't wander that far from my ancestors.

A Pronunciation Key

Fans of the International Phonetic Alphabet, I beg your forgiveness. Below is a do-it-myself list of names and places mentioned in the memoir.

Barone .... Bahr-own
Bonefro .... Bone-nay-fro
Campobasso........... Cahm-poh-bah-so
Eufemia................. You-fee-me-ah (in English, rhymes with "Bohemia")
Eh-ew-femme-ya (in Italian, rhymes with "Word stolen from Greeks")
Femia .... Femma-ya
Gennaro................. Jenn-ah-roh
Lucia .... Lew-chee-ah
Michelantonio .... Me-kale-ahn-tone-knee-oh
Molise .... Mo-leez
Paesani.................. Pie-sah-knee
Sapooch .... Sah-pooch

About the Author

Eufemia Fantetti, a graduate of SFU's Writer's Studio and the University of Guelph's MFA in Creative Writing program, is a three-time winner of *Accenti Magazine's* annual competition. Her work appears in *Event Magazine*, *The New Quarterly* and the *Globe and Mail* and is listed as notable by the Best American Essays Series. Fantetti is also an award-winning playwright and former stand-up comic. She teaches writing at Humber College and edits for the *Humber Literary Review*. Her debut book, *A Recipe for Disaster & Other Unlikely Tales of Love*, runner-up for the 2013 Danuta Gleed Literary Award and winner of the 2014 F.G. Bressani Literary Prize for short fiction, is also available from Mother Tongue Publishing.